REVISITING THE FOUNDATION OF MARRIAGE

Embracing Divine Principles for a

Successful Marriage

archbishop
GLORIA GRACE

ELYON HOUSE PUBLICATIONS

REVISITING THE FOUNDATION OF MARRIAGE

FIRST EDITION

Copyright 2014
Gloria Grace

ISBN-13: 978-0692304495
ISBN-10: 0692304495
PRINTED IN THE UNITED STATES OF AMERICA

Archbishop Gloria Grace is available for speaking appointments.

CONTACT INFORMATION

Email: hispriestlybride@gmail.com
www.messianictemple.net

TABLE OF CONTENTS

Chapter 8

PRAYERS

CONCLUSION

ABOUT THE AUTHOR

DEDICATION

This book is dedicated to my ultimate Bridegroom; the LORD Jesus Christ Who shed His last drop of Blood to make me His Bride. Many fires cannot quench His love. To Him I owe my love, my adoration and all my praise and worship. He is worthy!

INTRODUCTION

If the foundation be destroyed, what will the righteous do? (Psalm 11:3). Every institution, life, building, and organization has a foundation. The Bible says that a foolish man built his house on the sand, and when storm, flood and wind came against it, it fell and great was its fall. A wise man however, built his house on the rock and when the storm, the flood and the wind came against it, it did not fall because the foundation of the house was strongly founded upon the rock (Mathew 7: 24-28). The only sure foundation to any life, kingdom, throne, and institution, such as marriage, on which they will survive, is the foundation of the word of God. When temptations, challenges, and trials come, the house (marriage, government, and kingdom) stays strong, because it is founded upon the solid rock, which is the LORD Jesus Christ.

Marriage is ordained and executed by God. It is his original idea and the most important institution in the world. It started from the beginning of creation and will continue until the end of creation when the LORD Jesus will remove his Bride, the Church, from Earth.

The meaning and purpose of marriage have been misunderstood, that is why many people violently die in it or get confused and frustrated along the way. I once read a book by Myles Munroe while in Nigeria: In Pursuit of Purpose where he says that, when we do not understand why we are into something that is, the purpose for something, we abuse it. If a man for instance, does not understand why he is given a million dollars, he will abuse it, because he does not understand the purpose or the reason why that money was put into his hands. So he will waste it in things that don't have value and will be surprised that it is gone. He may end up into poverty again. In the same way, when couples don't understand why they are in marriage, they abuse their relationship. They will start fighting over money, clothes, toothpaste until they hurt each other. This book will look into the foundation –the original purpose of marriage and how it is part of divine purpose on Earth. The understanding of this will help couples have a vision and walk according to their vision in marriage because, without vision, according to God's word, people perish.

PROLOGUE

This book was written from the perspective of the challenges and trials some marriages pass through; why many marriages break and how to fulfill divine purpose for a marriage. Many marriages do not survive the heavy weight of traditions imposed upon them especially as one's spouse sets up his/her mind to live by traditional norms rather than by the word of God. Also, when one of the couple does not live out his/her marital responsibilities or live in harmony with the spouse, they miss divine purpose for their marriage. It may not survive. Traditional influence for instance, gave me lots of insights on how tradition penetrated even the Body of Christ, creating many pressures and unhappy experiences in many homes. The experiences described in the book are only meant to help couples learn to appreciate each other, fight for their marriages, build their families on the word of God- the foundation God established it, and ultimately fulfill God's purposes for their families and children. Tradition or certain unfavorable choices couples make ultimately affect the children and their future. Many school bullies and teenage suicides are a result of dysfunctions in families, and the children act them out among their peers or through some rebellious acts, which eventually get them into trouble except the mercy of God prevails for them. This book is enriched with wealth of experiences drawn from my marital journey and what I observed in other people's marriages. Let the Holy Spirit with His gifts of wisdom, knowledge, council, might and counsel endow and enrich these gifts upon every couple who want to live by divine principles for successful home. May the grace of our LORD Jesus Christ be upon every home that is set to live by the will of God, amen!

Chapter 1

MARRIAGE: GOD'S IDEA

The Bible opened, starting with these words: "In the beginning God made heaven and Earth". But the Earth was empty, void, and formless. According to the word of God, darkness was over the surface of the Earth (Genesis 1: 1-2). He was going to turn a useless, empty situation around and beautifully create and load it with exceeding beauty and life. So He began to speak things into existence. Within six days (of Earthly timing which could be different from God's timing since a day before God is one thousand years), He was done creating and loading the Earth. Now, someone was needed to take charge of it: to till the ground, tame the animals, mentor and dominate everything, and above all dwell in unity of fellowship and oneness with God.

> *...and there was no man to till the ground; but a mist went up from the earth and watered the whole face of the ground. And the LORD God formed man of the dust of the ground, and breathed into his nostrils the breath of life; and man became a living being (Genesis 2:4-7). And the LORD God took the man, and put him into the Garden of Eden to dress it and to keep it... And the LORD God said, it is not good that the man should be alone; I will make him an help meet for him (Genesis 2: 4-7; 15-18)*

Let's read on:

And Adam gave names to all cattle, and to the fowl of the air and to every beast of the field; but for Adam there was not found a help meet for him. And the LORD God caused a deep sleep to fall upon Adam, and he slept: and he took one of his ribs, and closed up the flesh instead thereof; And the rib, which the LORD God had taken from man, made he a woman, and brought her unto the man. And Adam said, 'this is now bone of my bones, and flesh of my flesh: she shall be called Woman, because she was taken out of Man'. Therefore, shall a man leave his father and his mother, and shall cleave unto his wife: and they shall be one flesh. And they were both naked, the man and his wife, and were not ashamed (Genesis 2: 21-25).

The above verse summed up the entire purpose of God in ordaining the institution of marriage. He caused a deep sleep to fall upon Adam, opened a place near his heart (surgery), and took out one of his ribs, formed a woman and closed up the place again. As soon as Adam got up from sleep, he recognized her as the bone of his bone and flesh of his flesh. He embraced her and called her Woman, because she was taken out of Man. And then the word of God continues: Therefore, shall a man leaves his father and his mother, and shall cleave unto his wife and they shall be one flesh. And they were both naked, the man and the wife and were not ashamed. From the verses above, we shall build the entire purpose and success of marriage.

Chapter 2

UNDERSTANDING GOD'S PURPOSE IN MARRIAGE

FOR COMPANIONSHIP

Malachi 2: 14: 15 says,

the LORD has been witness between you and the wife of your youth, With whom you have dealt treacherously; Yet she is your companion And your wife by covenant. But did He not make them one, Having a remnant of the Spirit? And why one? He seeks godly offspring

When God created everything on Earth, He made male and female but there was no help-meet for Adam - no companion. He was alone, and in need of a companion. In Ecclesiastes 4: 9-12 it is written:

Two are better than one, because they have a good reward for their labor. For if they fall, one will lift up his companion. But woe to him who is alone =when he falls, For he has no one to help him up. Again, if two lie down together, they will keep warm; but how can one be warm alone? Though one may be overpowered by another, two can withstand him. And a threefold cord is not quickly broken.

In this contest, we see that one of the reasons why God ordained marriage is for companionship. It is therefore understandable that, one of the major reasons why some marriages begin to fall apart is when one person begins to find a reason to stay away from the other, though still living in the same house or different places. Some men here in the USA or some western worlds, who have wives abroad deliberately leave them there for one reason or the other, and they stay all by themselves, yet they are married. I am not talking about the situation when there is a visa problem to bring them together. I am referring to those who have opportunities to bring their spouses to be with them, but for whatever reasons known to them, they want to stay apart. Besides, I have also met some well to do women who would tell me that they do not worry about staying away from their husbands because, they are comfortable where they are. Many families however, agree that they could stay in different nations: "you make money, bring home, I will take care of the children here" … and on and on" or since you are doing very well where you are and I am doing the same where I am, we can stay apart and probably visit one another during vacations. I know a man whose case is the later because his wife is doing exceedingly well financially where she is and he does not want to mess such a chance. So they stay apart while the wife stays with the children where she is. The LORD God, who made the man, said that it is not good for a man to be alone. I will make him a help meet for him. Couples are meant to stay together.

Another way the couple could be apart is that, some spouses get so engrossed in their businesses and jobs that they simply starve the other of their presence even though they still live together. In marriage, each person wants to see the other as more important than anything that occupies the other. Whenever something else however, whether friend, mother or even job/business/ministry takes the place of the spouse in the other person's life, the other party suffers loneliness. This loneliness is deep which is resulted from a sense of disconnection. In most of these cases, the children also suffer much emotional and psychological emptiness because, they need the missing parent. We will address this issue again later.

Separation can also be seen in the situation where the couple live together, but have almost nothing to do with each other. They are gradually growing apart and so have no interest in doing anything together - no quality time together, no vacation together, or even to be together on the dinner table. In some cases, one avoids the other's presence and so, constantly gets too busy with "anything" at all. When I mean anything, it could be too much working out, too much beautifying oneself always standing on the mirror, or too much attachment to phone, always on the phone with someone else where they could spend hours each day talking about anything, including businesses. That has become the person's comfort zone, rather than the spouse. In such a situation, the enemy will start filling in the gap that has been created by the emotional or physical absence of the other with irritations, anger, bitterness, complaints and hate. We shall talk about quality time later.

Couples need to understand that marriage is for companionship, and they need to make every effort in all circumstances to complement each other with their presence. Nothing, including money can replace the need of each other in one's life. It helps each of the couples to be sensitive to the needs of the other, and be a support. It is amazing if one of the couples could say that he did not know that the other was going through some emotional trauma or stress until she walks out. That's because, there was no sensitivity to the other's need, and this is caused by the absence of the other whether emotional -, or physical absence on consistent basis. Togetherness and companionship however, brings a sense of fulfillment, joy and creativity. I will recommend Gary Chapman's book, Five Love Languages to every married couple. He described five basic love languages. One can understand how to fulfill his/her spouse need for love by identifying how to speak the spouse's love language, and fulfill his emotional need for love. These love languages are: words of encouragement or praise, acts of service, giving gifts, physical touch and quality time. Each man or woman will be identified in one or two of these areas and speaking your spouse's love language by identifying his/her need and filling in the gap on consistent basis will draw out the best in each other. Most at times, you might be speaking a wrong love language to your spouse and be wondering why you are not pleasing him/her. But understanding the emotional need of your companion for love whether it is spending quality time with him/her, or words of encouragement/admiration, or physical touch (hugs, kisses, holding hands, sex), or helping out in acts of services: cleaning, fixing things up in the house, and so forth or simply gift giving no matter how small, will help you fulfill that need and bring fulfillment and joy to him or her. Yet you can only understand that emotional need for love when you are always there for each other.

PROCREATION OF GODLY SEED

Besides the need for companionship in marriage, God needed the procreation of godly human race. The procreation of godly offspring is so important to Him that He divinely intervenes in the issue of marriage, making the man and the woman one flesh. In His relationship with Abraham, having tried and found him faithful, the LORD God fully trusted

Him to raise godly offspring for Him. He said concerning the later:

> *For I know him, that he will command his children and his household after him, and they shall keep the way of the LORD, to do justice and judgment; that the LORD may bring upon Abraham that which he hath spoken of him (Genesis 18:19).*

He established a covenant with Abraham and it was not until He found Abraham faithful to carry on a godly heritage did He fulfill the promise of the promised seed. God wants couples, who will teach their children His way and continue His name for generations to come.

> *Give ear, O my people, to My law; incline your ears to the words of My mouth. I will open my mouth in a parable; I will utter dark sayings of old: Which we have heard and known, and our fathers have told us. We will not hide them from their children showing to the generation to come the praises of the LORD, and His strength, and His wonderful works that He hath done. For he established a testimony in Jacob and appointed a law in Israel, which he commanded our fathers, that they should make them known to their children: That the generation to come might know them, even the children which should be born; who should arise and declare them to their children (Psalm 78: 1-7).*

> *Only be careful, and watch yourselves closely so that you do not forget the things*

your eyes have seen or let them fade from your heart as long as you live. Teach them to your children and to their children after them (Deuteronomy. 4:9)

In Joshua 5:5-7, the LORD commanded Joshua saying:

. . . and take you up every man of you a stone upon his shoulder, according unto the number of the tribes of the children of Israel: that this may be a sign among you, that when your children ask their fathers in time to come, saying, What mean these stones? Then ye shall answer them, That the waters of Jordan were cut off before the ark of the Covenant of the LORD; . . . and these stones shall be for a memorial unto the children of Israel forever.

I consider myself privileged to be raised by godly parents and to be brought up under the ministry of Assemblies of God, because of the thorough way they taught us the Word right from childhood. It was a great foundation, which has helped me greatly through every hard experience I have had, both as a mother, a wife, a single parent and a woman of God. By God's grace, I have been teaching my children as I was thought, and they are filled with the fear and knowledge of the word of God. They are identifying their divine purposes and God is equipping each of them to fulfill His call upon their lives.

Our God expects parents to train their children in the way they should go, and such generation will raise up another generation that fears Him and impact their generation and so forth. When a generation fails to teach her children the word of God, or raise them in the way they should go, the next generation will not be able to carry on the godly seed or to continue in the fear of God. The difference between a mass murderer and a great man of God depends on godly or ungodly parenting. And these two generations do raise after their kinds unless someone in the godless generation begins to seek after - and find God. We do hear or experience a national leader who mass-murders the people he led, or who declares war against the entire world; on the other hand, we do see great men of God whom the LORD use to touch lives and save millions from spending eternity in Hell. It's mostly about parenting, or the grace of God could reach someone and he/she surrenders to God in spite of parenting. The LORD God therefore, seeks couples/parents that will raise godly offspring for Him.

The devil however, is very interested in marriage unions and family issues in order to perform his mission of stealing, killing and destroying. This is why many homes are under a severe attack. It is therefore very appropriate to seek the face of God for the right marriage partner, who will be in one accord with you as you face the storms of life together, and also raise the godly offspring the LORD is seeking out of your unions. (See my book: Before You Get Married).

It is very necessary to point out that, that a marriage is divinely instituted or that God supernaturally provided a man with a wife just as He did for Isaac in the case of finding Rebecca for him, does not exempt a home from going through an attack or the devil attempting to kill the godly offspring produced in that marriage. We read about how in order to kill Jesus at birth, King Herod mass-murdered children two years and under, but for the obedience and wisdom of Joseph and Mary to escape with Jesus by night, to Egypt. The enemy seeks to destroy that godly seed, or to stop the seed from being born, or even to distract the seed by creating unnecessary war and troubles into such families. Faith however, overcomes.

Isaac, being the promised seed that would carry on the godly heritage and the covenant race that God promised Abraham, married Rebecca by divine provision. But the first challenge they had was that Rebecca could not conceive. She was barren, just as Sarah; Abraham's wife. She was barren until the LORD supernaturally gave them Isaac through their faithfulness.

Rebecca could not conceive for twenty years. Isaac therefore, entreated the LORD for her and the LORD heard him and opened her womb (Genesis 25:21). If you start a journey of faith with God it is only by faith, when the LORD has perfected your faith and found you faithful and trustworthy, that He releases the covenant promise. You are not to apply sense knowledge, but keep holding unto the LORD until He fulfills that promise. Perhaps Isaac would not take up a second wife, because of his father's mistake with Hagar which brought forth Ishmael, and so he patiently awaited the godly offspring God was seeking through their union that would carry on the covenant promise. That godly offspring would come only in response to prayer and faith just as Hannah had to have Prophet Samuel only through prayer and vow. Isaac's parents had him only through faith, patience and consistent obedience to divine instructions. God needs our cooperation, our patients and walk of faith. The promised seed comes only through travail, faith and obedience to divine instructions.

When the LORD opened the womb of Rebecca and they
had the two nations: "their twin children", they began to play favoritism and became dishonest to each other. In spite of it, the LORD was choosing out of the twins the one that would carry on the covenant promise of Abraham to the next generation.

Esau the first born like Isaac his father, who favored

him, loved his stomach above God's plan and purpose. He sold his birthright to Jacob for a bowl of food. He also neglected God's covenant with his father and married strange (Canaanite) women, who brought too much distresses to their family. On the other hand, Jacob wanted to carry on the covenant promise of God at all costs, probably because his mother who favored him taught him the need to hold unto eternal things. Rebecca might also have shared with him the word of the prophecy she received during pregnancy concerning them which says: "the elder shall serve the younger" (Genesis 25:23), hence the word of God that says: "Esau I hate and Jacob I loved" (Malachi 1:3; Romans 9:13). Rebecca therefore, was going to walk in deceit for the fulfillment of this prophecy over Jacob's life. And so, she deceived her blind husband, Isaac so that he blessed Jacob in place of Esau, whom he planned to bless in spite of God's word. Still, through deceit, in a bid to protect Jacob from being hurt by Esau, who threatened to kill him for stealing his blessing; she helped him escape to her kinsmen convincing her husband that she would not like Jacob to marry from these Canaanite women because, had brought much distress to them. So with cunning and wisdom, she helped Jacob take the right decision to go and marry among her kinsmen rather than the Canaanite women, submitting to the will of God. She also helped him move towards the right direction until he obtained the promise that was meant for him and his generation. Thus, God found the godly offspring he sought out of the union of Isaac and Rebecca.

As the LORD continued to seek the godly offspring for Jacob's generation, we saw another great family dysfunction, which however He turned around for good. Jacob the deceiver, now being deceived by his father in-law Laban, ended up marrying two sisters (Rachel and Leah) who strove with each other while Jacob was playing favoritism with the one he loved, Rachel. Their dysfunction continued even as they were giving their maidens, Zilpar and Bilah to him to help them produce more sons on their behalves for their husband. Thus, Jacob had four women bearing children for him, not as he originally planned. He originally planned to marry only Rachel, but by the deceit of Laban their father, he ended up with both sisters through whom the LORD God would fulfill His purpose of seeking godly offspring that would fulfill His ultimate eternal purpose of birthing the twelve tribes of Israel and bring Messiah into the world for the salvation of the world. God was raising and establishing a covenant and a holy nation out of this family. Jacob was in His will. Thus, in spite of the dysfunctions of Jacob's family, the LORD was able to raise a godly/priestly generation and nation through which He would fulfil His ultimate purpose of bringing the Savior for the salvation of the whole world for in spite of its dysfunction, Jacob was teaching his children the ways of the LORD.

As he however, played the same game of favoritism his parents played which created strife between him and Esau his brother, his sons hated Joseph whom he loved above others and sold him into slavery. But the LORD had already prepared Joseph through the word of God that Jacob taught him and from what he observed from his father in regards to his relationship with God, before he was taken away. He was sustained by the fear of the LORD. Joseph was tried and he suffered greatly for his faith in God, until the LORD found him faithful and raised him as the second in command in Egypt for the preservation of the godly generation (the nation) he sought out of the union of Jacob and his wives. That nation is Israel, the name the LORD gave him after he wrestled and prevailed with an Angel of God, whom he would never let go for an entire night till morning when the LORD had to bless him for his faith.

Jacob was able to pass onto his sons the fear and the covenant of God before he died. This sustained the entire generation of Jacob in Egypt until, through Moses, the LORD delivered them from Egyptian bondage. He brought them out as His army and His Priests into the Promised Land, the land that flowed with milk and honey. The purpose of God in raising godly offspring, a godly generation and a priestly nation was fulfilled. Through that covenant, all the seed of the Earth were engrafted into God through the LORD Jesus Christ, the Promised Seed of the woman that would crush the serpent's head. He was the seed of Abraham in the flesh.

Couples could go through many difficult experiences at times, including some period of childlessness, which they can only survive through hope in the promise that God gave them, and faith in God. This is because, He sought out of your unions His own seed, and the enemy wants to kill that seed of God you carry, or would not want you to patiently wait upon Him to see the manifestation of His promised seed in your unions. Some of such seeds could also bring some periods of heartache to the parents, which usually provokes consistent prayers and intercession for such a child until he gets hold of God's plan for his own life. The enemy's war against such a seed is not just on the seed, but against the plan of God on Earth through such a seed. Whatever trials and testing a couple encounter, it is always important to know that it is through faith and patience that we obtain the promises of God. We can always overcome through His grace.

My marriage with my husband was by divine revelation. I could say that the LORD achieved one purpose through our union: the godly offspring He planned through our union. We were not anything like each other.

We never met each other or heard about each other until the LORD revealed him to me in a dream. According to him, he was in a Church at Alabama when he received the message concerning me. I was a student in the University of Calabar, Nigeria at the time and he was starting his second degree program as an Environmental Engineer with Howard University, Washington DC. After four years of struggles in communication and hardship, fasting and prayers, we eventually met and wedded in Lagos following divine instruction to wed where I was at the time, but not according to the expectation of his people. They would not attend the wedding. They wanted it to happen in their village. According to him later on, if we had taken the wedding to the village, it would not hold. Even in Lagos where we had it, it took place only by a supernatural work of God produced by great faith, and prayers and fasting. His people did not appreciate the way we wedded. It did not sit well with them, but he returned to the US after a brief visit with them, and I stayed in Nigeria for another five years because of visa problem and for "whatever reasons".

The marriage was an extremely difficult experience, because of the influence of his brother and his people over his life. He decided he wanted to make peace with his people regarding the wedding. That peace was going to be very disastrous to our marriage because it would mean total union with his people at the cost of the marriage. According to him, a popular man of God prophesied to him as a student in High school that God would use him to establish his people. So, his people became his priority.

The LORD Jesus said in Mathew 10:34:

> *Think not that I am come to send peace on earth: I came not to send peace, but a sword. For I am come to set a man at*

variance against his father, and the daughter against her mother, and the daughter in law against her mother in law.

The word of God is a sword that divides the natural order and brings in the order of God into a situation. It is up to us to choose if we will allow divine order or natural order to take place in our lives and families. Divine order in marriage requires that a man leaves his family and cleaves to his wife (it means giving priority to his new family above his extended family).

A year after our wedding, he visited home again. Right at the airport as I was coming to welcome him, he announced to me of his intention to send me to live with his people. He was acting on the influence of his people based on the unity he said he has with them. It was not his decision. I cried, begged, grieved and even cursed, because I already had encountered his people several times before our wedding and knew it would be a bitter experience. Besides, they were not happy the way we wedded. It was not the best decision to make at the time, but nothing I said or did changed his mind. He had made up his mind never to do anything that would tamper with his unity with them again.

Living with his people, which also was the period of my first pregnancy was not easy. I suffered too much as he could not do anything with me without consulting them. It was a great trying time for me.

When my first baby, Miracle was born, all Hell broke loose for her entrance into the world. In Revelation 20, the woman was pregnant and the dragon awaited the birth of the baby, to swallow him. That was exactly my experience with the birth of my daughter, the first godly offspring the LORD sought out of our union. Her conception and name came through announcement and revelation during a seven-day fasting and prayer (See my first book: ***How Do We Invest In Our Children?***). Shortly before her birth, the LORD began to prepare me through many revelations, prophecies, and warnings for the great storm awaiting me at her birth. It was great ocean waves splashing me from every direction, while I stood steadfastly on the Rock in the middle of the ocean calling out: "Jesus, Jesus, Jesus". The devil never intended that godly offspring to be born, or exist.

I suffered birth pangs in the hospital for three days and nights of induced labor without food. Without anyone's approval the doctor carried out a C-section. Miracle had turned yellow. Her survival was a miracle. Both of us spent two weeks in the hospital within which I was denied proper food (the feeding was carried out by one's relatives, but the in-laws would not contact my people). I was fed a cup of black Lipton tea with a tasteless small wrapped corn starch, each day. I was like a skeleton in bed, with no proper breast milk to feed my baby, while I was expected to die. I laid facing the roof, unable to rise up by myself. That was the enemy's first attempt to take me away from her so that I would not be able to raise her in the way she should go; an attempt to thwart the will of God for her life.

One night in my affliction, I had a serious fight with the spirit of death. Someone visited me that day and fervently prayed for me. At night, I had a dream. I realized in my dream that I was in a room and a bed dedicated to the spirit of death. In real situation, anyone that entered that room in that hospital and passed a night on that bed died except by divine intervention. So I was ushered into the room after they removed a Principal of Assemblies of God Bethel Seminary High School, who died there. I did not know about that when they were transferring me into that ward. There was a conspiracy to do away with me and take the baby away.

I spent the entire two weeks in that room under a serious infection on my operated womb that would not heal, but completely opened up my wound. My womb was open again. During the fight with the spirit of death in the dream, which I cast out of that room, confessing that wherever the sole of my feet treads is my possession, I had a confrontation with someone–one of the people caring for me. He insisted there in that dream that the spirit of death must come in, but I already cast it out. The LORD began to reveal to me as I opened my eyes (unconsciously praying in tongues) on why I had been there for too long. My wound was spiritually being poisoned every day, and I was not expected to get out alive. He also revealed to me about the difficulty my husband was having in taking decisions for our family because of his brother's stronghold on him. He could not do anything without his approval. Besides, I kept seeing the craze to take the baby from me. At this point, I rose from the bed where I had been lying like a corpse completely malnourished, looking like a skeleton for the past two weeks. The doctor, who all these while, left me to Nurses on training, finally entered the room. Someone unrelated to me had confronted him and threatened to take me out of there to a University Teaching Hospital. My body recovered instantly as I sent someone to buy me some nourishing food, and I was ready to go through another surgery over my opened womb.

This second surgery nearly took my life. When I cast the spirit of death out of the room in that dream, two people in the open-ward died. I was scared and so I asked the doctor not to put me to sleep through the next surgery. While on the stretcher, I watched the doctor cut me with a razor blade over and over, and I felt the raw pains of razor slicing my flesh, cutting off old wounds to make way for a new stitching together of my flesh. I bled profusely and the worst was that, of all the five large hooked needles the doctor was using to sew my flesh together, four of them broke each time he tried pushing the needle through the old healed wounds remaining only one more needle. It was Sunday evening. If that one had broken, I would have bled to death and they would not have any more needle to stitch me together. So at the breaking of the fourth needle, I busted out in tears on the surgery stretcher, remembering my husband and my parents, who no one would contact for me; or being surrounded by unlovely faces, who said that I wedded their brother. But the mercy of the LORD prevailed for me and I survived. All these happened, because a godly offspring was born, and the enemy would not want this godly family to be established.

My survival caused more agonizing pains for me as they continued to take the worst decisions over my life and that of Miracle. Miracle died in my hands twice during this period of our sufferings which continued for a couple of years, but the LORD raised her back to life as I cried to Him for mercy. Refer to my book: *How Do We Invest In Our Children?*

Every suffering Miracle and I suffered even unto death was partly because, Miracle, a godly offspring was born and the devil wanted her dead or imbecile. She could not walk because of lack of calcium (that comes from milk) which they denied her at birth and early months. I sought the face of God for seven days through dry fasting when she was about eighteen months old and she got up and started walking (See my book, above). Today, she is completing her first degree, aspiring for a medical career. She is also getting ready to be ordained as a minister, the beginning of the fulfillment of her calling as a Prophet unto nations. The devil completely lost the battle over her -, and my life. But it was a journey of faith, endurance and perseverance.

The enemy severely attacks many marriages in order

to crush them and thwart the plan of God in raising the godly offspring He sought out of the unions. Couples therefore, need to work out their salvation in marriage through fear and trembling, in following divine instructions for marriage in order to stay under divine protection and provision. He is very faithful to see you through. You don't have to go through certain hardships if the two can be of one mind and support each other. It is only through love, patience and fear of God that couples learn to overcome. I suffered very much in my marriage to the point of homelessness with Miracle because my husband could not stand for the marriage that we started with God, his people. In all the troubles I went through as the battering ram kept running after me and Miracle with an angry crushing speed, the LORD said to me: The hand of Zerubbabel laid the foundation of this house, and his hands shall finish it (Zachariah 4:9). We overcame. I do not want to go into too much details on this testimony to avoid distraction to our main focus here. It is written that many are the afflictions of the righteous, but the LORD shall deliver him from them all. He keeps all his bones, and not one of them shall be broken. The enemy will rage to a great length to destroy the godly seed, but the couple needs to stay focused and attentive to the LORD's instruction just as Joseph had to escape with Jesus and Mary at night to Egypt to save the life of Jesus, following divine instruction. Parents are to not to take their marriage for granted, because the seed you are bringing into the world carries destiny of nations.

SEXUAL UNION

Another purpose of marriage, apart from companionship and procreation of godly offspring, is for sexual union between the two. In 1 Corinthians 7: 5 Paul says:

Do not withhold yourselves from each other unless you agree to do so just for a set time, in order to devote yourselves to prayer. Then you should come together again so that Satan does not tempt you through your lack of self-control.

Sexual union of the husband and wife is very important to God, because through that means, He establishes the godly offspring as we discussed earlier. It is also the way that God achieved his one flesh union between the man and the woman. In 1 Corinthians 16: 16 it is written: Or do you not know that the one who joins himself to a prostitute is one flesh with her? For He says, "THE TWO SHALL BECOME ONE FLESH." So through sexual union of the man and his wife, they are one flesh, and because they are joined to the LORD, they become one spirit with God. The two who are one flesh are also joined to the LORD as one spirit: But the one who joins himself to the LORD is one spirit with Him (Verse 17). So, the three-fold-chords is not easily broken. God made you and your spouse one flesh in Him.

When however, separation begins to take place in a marriage order than the circumstance that is permitted by God (because such circumstance is beyond the couple's control), such separation is not the will of God. Some people do it in order to have enough and un-challenging time to freely do what they want to do without the other knowing about it. They come up with so many lies in order to continue to keep their spouses away from them either in a distant land, or emotionally keep them away from themselves. In this case, it is a manipulative way of putting their wives or husbands away which God says that he hates. In King James Version of Malachi 2: 16, it is written that the LORD says that He hates putting away. The separation creates absence of sexual union which supposed to keep them together as one flesh. In such circumstance, except by the mercy of God, certain things begin to occupy the hole that is created by that separation.

God wants the husband and wife to enjoy their bodies, enjoy the union of each other and the companionship of each other for this is well pleasing to Him. Through their union in Him, and through their sexual union which pleases Him, He blesses them with children who will serve and glorify Him on Earth. Unity in all aspects of the marriage is power and attracts the presence of God in such union. Because the unity is in Him, nothing shall be impossible with the two for the Bible says that one shall chase a thousand, but two shall put ten thousand to flight.

TO AVOID THE SIN OFFORNICATION

One other reason for marriage union is that God wants to keep His people out of the sin of fornication or sexual immorality. When we talk about fornication, we are talking about a very serious sin. Fornication is sexual immorality between two unmarried individuals, but adultery is the same sin but with married individuals. It also includes incest, lechery and all kinds of sexual sins and lustful desires. Our bodies are the temple of God, and the Spirit of God dwells in us. God wants us to keep our bodies pure, but He judges or destroys people who defile the temple of God, the body. One of the ways one can defile one's body is through the sin of fornication. In 1 Corinthians 6: 18, the LORD warns us to flee from sexual immorality. Every other sin a person commits is outside the body, but the sexually immoral person sins against his own body. It is also written:

It is reported commonly that there is
fornication among you, and such fornication

as is not so much as named among the Gentiles, that one should have his father's wife (1 Corinthians 5: 1)

But the fearful, and unbelieving, and the abominable, and murderers, and whoremongers, and sorcerers, and idolaters, and all liars, shall have their part in the lake which burneth with fire and brimstone: which is the second death (Rev. 5: 8)

Mortify therefore your members which are upon the earth; fornication, uncleanness, inordinate affection, evil concupiscence, and covetousness, which is idolatry (Col 3:5).

But fornication, and all uncleanness, or covetousness, let it not be once named among you, as becometh saints ;(Ephesians 5:3)

Nevertheless, to avoid fornication, let every man have his own wife, and let every woman have her own husband (1 Corinthians 7:2).

The LORD God created us with sexual instincts, which He meant to be limited within the boundaries of marriage unions, as we noted above. But the enemy uses this instinct in man to turn Him against the commands of the LORD, and so we see various types of sexual sins and perversions in the world today as described above which, in turn, destroys man and turns him to Hell.

The LORD understands that man would misuse this gift, and so He made a way of escape for him: Nevertheless, to avoid fornication, let every man have his own wife, and let every woman have her own husband (as above).

So then, sex within the bounds of marriage, apart from the purpose of reproduction, also produces a deep expression of love, pleasure, emotional and psychological fulfillment. It also creates emotional bonding that keeps the couple together emotionally and wanting to be with each other at all times. The fulfillment experienced through sexual union, keeps the individual couples in creative and harmonious living. It also keeps the couple from the dangers of exposure to living in sexual immorality, the judgment of God and ultimately, dangers of Hell. There is something I need to mention here, which the LORD taught me concerning a healthy sex life.

Just as sex produces life, it can also produce death even within marriage unions. A man who is deeply in love with his wife as Christ loved the church and gave Himself for her, wants to express himself to his wife deeply and intimately through non-verbal, but deep expressions of love. He is actually pouring his life, his love, his being into his wife as one flesh, sharing the entirety of his life with her through sexual union. That is a one flesh union. They are one, flowing into each other both physically, emotionally, spiritually and psychologically.

On the other hand, however, if a man hates his wife in his heart, despises her or degrades her, curses and verbally abuses her, that is what he expresses to her or rather pours inside her during sex. Rather than becoming edified, creative and sharpened emotionally and spiritually as it ought to be, she becomes unlively, depressed and gradually fading away. That is death. And when she is sexually abused, she becomes abused also emotionally, physically, spiritually and psychologically. This way, her life will begin to be torn down gradually until either the two of them or she recognizes that she is being destroyed and does something about it.

That union was gradually separated from Christ through the demeaning and evil attitude of one of the partners, and so it begins to produce a gradual death, instead of life.

The LORD revealed two things to me in the area of the use of abusive languages in marriage, twice. When couples begin to curse each other, or one curses the other, they begin to pollute the foundation of their marriage which was laid in Christ. The evil seed sown on that foundation, the curse-words will begin to germinate and grow, and gradually begin to suffocate/destroy the life of that marriage or whoever is being attacked. At other time, He showed me the marriage covenant standing between a couple and holding them together, but with curses or abusive language, they tear it down leaving the marriage with nothing to hold it together. It is a matter of time. The abusive language is like a bad taste or venom to the foundation of the marriage and therefore repels each of the couple from the other, even sexually. It is written that a good man out of the good treasure of his heart brings forth good; and an evil man out of the evil treasure of his heart brings forth evil. For out of the abundance of the heart his mouth speaks (Luke 6: 45). When verbal abuse and demeaning words begin to happen in a marriage, it begins from the heart of the abuser, who already in his/her heart has started demeaning the other. Such a heart therefore has nothing pleasant or life to give in the area of sexual union from which life flows together and also procreates (for more information on the use of tongue, check out my book: God Hears, God Answers).

It is therefore required that the couple come together before God, confess whatever they have against each other as soon as the enemy begins to bring bad thoughts against each other. They also need to spend quality time with each other so they can have a healthy relationship and a healthy sexual life. Healthy sexual life will cause them to produce spiritually, emotionally and psychologically healthy children and they can have great positive lives and family. These can only be achieved by following the pattern the LORD mapped out for marriage.

Before we round up this topic, we will need to touch the importance of communication. Healthy communication includes communication from the heart. When we talk about communication, we are referring to communication that involves different forms of expressions between the couple which includes eye contact, facial expressions and body moves. The Bible says the two shall be one flesh. When one looks at the other and observes certain moves, he/she responds in a positive way to take care of what the other needs.

Besides those moves, verbal communication needs to be from the heart. The word of God says from the abundance of the heart the mouth speaks. So, when the communication comes from the pureness of heart, especially a heart that is filled with the Spirit of God and with the word of God, there is a flow of life from one to another through communication. It also brings the same flow of life during sexual union. When the heart lies, and communication is deceitful, it also will cause an unhealthy sex life for there is no free flow of life as well as free flow of information. There is therefore need for transparency in communication for the edification of each other, for overall support of each other. Healthy sexual life is healthy marriage and healthy life of the children, the godly offspring in the marriage. There is nothing impossible for the two for they are joined unto the LORD.

DANGERS OF SEPERATION IN MARRIAGE

We briefly addressed the issue of separation above.

Let's pay more attention to this subject. Separation in marriage could occur when the couple agrees to stay away from each other either by circumstances beyond their control or for whatever reasons they may have. We also mentioned other separations such as emotional separation, or avoiding each other. There is also a legal separation due to marital problems that might eventually lead to divorce in marriage. But let's focus on the separations that have nothing to do with marital split. From the warning of Apostle Paul in 1 Corinthians 7:5 where he stated:

> *Do not withhold yourselves from each other unless you agree to do so just for a set time, in order to devote yourselves to prayer. Then you should come together again so that Satan does not tempt you through your lack of self-control.*

We see that separation or denial of each person to the other results to temptation to start having extra-marital affairs. Many people today continue to languish in deep emotional pains and emptiness and some begin to experience some psychological traumas, because their help-meet or the man is not there. The pain of loneliness is too much and at times, unbearable. I was there for too many years. The reason is that the presence of each other complements the life and well-being of the other. In such a situation as loneliness, you notice one person drying up and nothing matters to him/her anymore because, part of his /her life is somewhere and no matter how much he/she tries to reach out for emotional help or support, the other party was not there. But thank God for technologies that has made communication very cheap and easy. International and video calls are getting cheaper and cheaper through some calling cards. That however, solves only a momentary emotional need for a little while; the person drains up again and needs the other. This has led to some secret extra-marital affairs among some couples who could not faithfully endure the loneliness. Remember that Paul said: ...lest the devil tempts your incontinency (lack of self-control). This will take us to the next paragraph.

Another danger of separation is that the other party may be distracted. I remember once in Nigeria, I mentioned to one Christian sister that I have a strong feeling that someone was distracting my husband from me in the USA. We just got wedded, my husband travelled and I stayed back in Nigeria trying to acquire visa to be with him in the US. I began to perceive over and over that someone was distracting my husband from me. I continued to pray about it, but the more I prayed the clearer I was seeing the situation continually. It was consistently pressed hard on me to fight for my marriage, and I did it with so much heartbreak until I prayed through the situation and obtained victory.

When I was praying and travailing in prayers over it, I mentioned the situation to a sister with whom I got myself acquainted in the Christian Private School where I was teaching at the time. She was also a child of God. Another day she approached me and said that when I said that someone was distracting my husband, she felt guilty because, she was in love with someone else apart from her husband. The situation with these two learned couple was that the man married his wife, took her abroad for further studies for both of them, came back and dumped her in the village to live with his people. He on the other hand, was a professor in the University about a three to four -hour drive from home. She, living in the village, was transporting herself to the city for the teaching job, every day. During weekends, she would go and be with him, and returns probably Monday morning straight to school or Sunday evening. So she was spending only about two to three days every week with her husband. In the meanwhile, she fell in love with another man where she was. The man held her heart. No one knew what the husband might be doing there since he was by himself –God knows- but I was not sure since I never heard anything concerning him.

This sister was never pregnant and she was continually staying far away from her husband. When she mentioned to me about her being in love with another man, I did not allow myself to listen to the details of her story. I cannot remember how the Holy Spirit led me to counsel her, but I made her understand that she was totally wrong and it was unacceptable before God and man. I also provided her with some books to help her in her Christian walk. As soon as she turned away from this life of hypocrisy (which I believed was caused by the misjudgment of her husband or his parents in the village), the LORD opened a door for her husband to study for his PHD in London. He left her behind and traveled. I believe that was on agreement, but hold on a minute! The LORD had suddenly opened her womb and she took in as soon as her husband was about to travel to London. He got there and sent her a letter by courier and asked her to resign from her job immediately and come over. That's how the LORD established that family. God elevated her life when she discovered her error and repented and turned back to the LORD. He reunited them as husband and wife and removed her from the village where she was playing the role of a decorated slave for her husband's people, blessed her with a fruit of the womb and sent her to live together with her husband abroad where they probably would want to give their baby the life they planned to give him/her. But the good thing is that they now live together as a family.

Besides the above listed problems, there are talents,

gifts and virtues that the LORD invested into the life of each person that will only become useful when he or she is together with the spouse. Because of separation however, the other person is frustrated and empty as he or she cannot do the things she needs to do to complement the other. The creativity is limited, because love and love making with your spouse generates strength and creativity on each other. You find yourself in one another, and whenever you are together, spending time with the other, you continue to spiritually partake of the likeness of each other. You are complete and fulfilled, because your union is in Christ in whom you are finding the fulfillment. His glory covers your union and His strength becomes your strength. That's why two is better than one. With your one-heart union, you emanate with indescribable strength and achieve far better than what one person achieves. One shall chase a thousand, but two shall put ten thousand to flight (Deuteronomy 32: 10;

     I did a business called 5Linx. It was a very lucrative video phone business. But I discovered in that business that most of the people who were on top of that business, succeeding so greatly were mainly couples who worked together. I checked out this Senior Vice President, he was consciously working together with the wife, and that one, the same, and so many of them. Yea, some single people made it to the top, but I saw far greater success among couples. I openly admired a lot of them, because of their unity. In ministries, when couples work together, they achieve greatly in soul winning and in the overall ministry committed into their hands. There has to be that unity because, God blesses the union and works closely with the unity of the couple. The LORD Jesus said to the Father in His prayers for the Church:

That they all may be one; as thou, Father,
art in me, and I in thee, that they also may

be one in us: that the world may believe that thou hast sent me And the glory which thou gavest me I have given them that they may be one, even as we are one ((John 17: 21-22).

And as one with the Father, He in the Father, the Son and the Holy Spirit will dwell as one with the unity of His body. The unity of the body of Christ starts with the unity of the husband and the wife. And then the LORD Jesus asked the Father to give to this unity of His body the very glory that He had with the Father. So the glory that is upon the union
of husband and wife is the very glory of Christ. That's why they operate and achieve unimaginable things and nothing can stop them: one, chasing a thousand, but two putting ten thousand to flight. This takes me to the issue of spending Time together. We will look on that later.

DANGERS OF SEPERATION ON THE CHILDREN

We are looking into this area, because "godly offspring" or children, is one of the reasons why God ordained marriage. That is why you are also one flesh with your spouse. So your presence in the lives of your children is part of God's plan. When I heard my first baby in Nigeria, I began to notice that she needed her father.

As early as four, five months, she would cry and cry and when a man picked her up, she would clasp herself on him and feel so comfortable that anyone around would notice the difference the presence and the hands of a father is to the baby. My heart grieved very much. I related the circumstance of her birth above. She was constantly looking at my face, and showing much understanding. She so understood. I kept assuring her that it would all be well.

As she grew into one year, the absence of a father in her life was affecting her and me very much. When her father later visited and left, one day a man picked her up from me and held her awhile. When he eventually gave her back to me, she began to cry as she watched the man go away. Each time I watched Maury Show here in the USA and watch these young ladies cry and wail, because they want the father of their son or daughter to physically get committed to their lives, I perfectly understand the situation. The situation with me was that my husband was in the USA and I was in Nigeria. That was because; I needed a visa to travel to join him over there. I suffered too much with our baby, part of what I described above because we were far from each other. But when we (my daughter and I) eventually came over here and she was united with her father, I was very much elated and fulfilled in that area of my life that my baby was now with her father. I watched her tell him story after story each day she came back from school, and did things she would not do with me which is part of the normal developmental process of a child, and which produces the emotional, psychological and physical well-being of such a child.

Many children consider their father's absence in their lives as not wanting them, or loving them. The boys would not have a role model that teaches them daily how to be a man, or even someone to discipline them with strong hands. Those who grow with the father but not with the mother do not have that nurturing love of mother that creates love and strength in them.

Generally, most of such children have suppressed anger within them and they often get into troubles in school and in various places. Some of them end up dead or killing someone to spend the rest of their lives in jail. That was because, their anger is turned inward and they often hurt someone they love or just anybody. Dad was not there, or was too busy or was separated. The girls whose self-esteem and emotional well-being are also supported by the father also consider themselves abandoned by their fathers. In all these, their lives are affected so much right from their formative years to adulthood, even into their own marital lives. Whatever seed you sow in your marital life, will manifest through your children. Be careful!

In Church at times, I watch some children from single mothers getting too attached to some men in the Church as they try to identify themselves with fathers. I understand the situation as I watched these children always come around some men, and tried playing with them. At times, they call them uncles, but some vulnerable innocent children have ended up dead or sexually abused by some of such men. The vulnerability of these children is because; they were trying to identify with male figures –father figures. God have mercy! Some boys are strong headed because of frustration. They are psychologically reacting to the absence of their fathers. Besides, some of those boys' attitude or girls' wildness could only be tamed by the strong hands of a man, not with the gentle nurturing love of the woman. Both the man and the woman have different roles to play in the development of a child. But thank God, who is Father to the fatherless, and mother to the motherless. David said: though my mother and my father forsake me, but the LORD shall take me up (Psalm 27: 10).

In situations where fathers and mothers could afford to be together (I mean in situations where the circumstance regarding their separation was not an -impossible one), let them come together as a family. If you feel that this one is making more money where he or she is, "let me stay here and support you from afar", then the purpose of the marriage has been defeated. Marriage is for togetherness and oneness, not for separation. If you take such decisions as being away for better living condition of your family, be sure to always spend time with them on phone especially video phones (thank God for Skype), and plan to visit them often. As soon as you have the opportunity to unite everyone together as a family, and not to be separated again, do it.

The absence of the father or mother in the lives of the children has a long time effect on the lives of such children even to adulthood, as I mentioned earlier. Most times when I watch movies and see some adults grieve over the lack of fathers in their lives, I feel terrible. Even as adults, they still need the dad that would tell them that he loves and cares about them. My father passed on to glory recently, but his maltreatments on me, lack of closeness and his constant abuses on me created a need in me to continue to press for his love even at this age until he recently went home. I continue to feel the emptiness his love would have filled in my life, instead of those demeaning words, abuses and wrong names he called me even into my adulthood. I continued to try to reach out to him. I continued to press in my adulthood to be part of him, to feel his fatherly love. That is part of the long time effect on the children, who feel the absence of their father in their lives, or their father was there but emotionally absent - not connected to them-, or he abused them. They could not reach out to him; they could not have the sense of belonging, security and warmness that exist between children and their fathers or mothers. They feel alone and that loneliness follows them and affects their relationship with men/women.

Some separations in marriages however, are healthy especially when one of the parents is violent or very abusive, and would not see any need to change. Here the abusive parent becomes a very bad influence on the children, and may even harm both the children and the other parent. Here the children will become confused, disorganized and even disoriented. In some other instances, they may start seeking the protection or acceptance, which they cannot find at home in wrong places. They may end up getting into troubles as young girls may start having boyfriends, who would start showing them the love they could not get from the parents and they may end up with early pregnancies, abortion or dropping out of school. The young men may start hanging out with wrong crowds doing drugs, and learning all kinds of wrong things from them. The violence at home begins to show in their relationship with people: boys beginning to display the same abuses they learned from their fathers to girls, while ladies could be falling into the hands of men that abuse them, seeing the abuse as their way of demonstrating their love to them. Separation is required in such abusive relationship if nothing can change the abusive parent. The girls see accepting abuses from the man as the way to relate to men, while boys will grow into abusive and violent men. In all cases, the lives of the children have been negatively impacted unless they are enrolled into counseling or therapies to help them to see the true or acceptable side of life. Read more on my book: *Why You Must Get out of Abuse (Not available yet).*

Chapter 3

MARRIAGE, A COVENANT

In Malachi 2:14, the LORD says, *Yet she is your companion, your wife by covenant*. Why is a marriage, made official? Why would it become such a great occasion where people would suspend their duties that day and all converge to witness the occasion of joining the man and the woman as husband and wife? It is a covenant. God was establishing an institution (a family) in the presence of witnesses. These witnesses are not only human beings, but are also God the Father, Son and the Holy Spirit and the presence of the multitude of His angels. In this occasion the woman and the man are made to recite some vows before these heavenly and Earthly witnesses such as:

> *I (name) take thee (name) to be my lawful wedded husband/wife, to have and to hold, from this day forward, for better, for worse, for richer, for poorer, in sickness and in health, to love and to cherish; till death do us part, according to God's holy ordinance and thereto I pledge thee my faith/myself to you (protestant wedding vows: wedding vows and readings).*

After the marriage vow, the couple is made to make one more vow before they exchange rings. Let's look at the symbol of ring in such a commitment. In many situations of life, ring is symbolic. Certain people, who get committed into some things wear ring as a symbol of their eternal commitment. Before they wear that ring, they make vows. In marriage, rings are symbolic of timeless commitment, love and the vows of the marriage. Let's look at some of those committed words spoken before the ring. Some words of such vows are as follows: *As this ring is round with no beginning and ending, so does my love and commitment to you have no beginning and ending....* This shows an endless and an unconditional love towards each other. It could also start with these words: *With this ring, I thee wed/ with my body, I thee honor-* showing commitment to marital faithfulness and holiness. *All my worldly goods, I thee endow...* This shows the commitment of your labor, inheritance and provision for each other. The Bible says in Matthew 12:37 ... by your words you will be justified, and by your words you will be condemned.

Many people casually recite these words like a cliché – something that has to be done as though it is not important. They see it as a tradition, not a commitment. So they run into this commitment without knowing what they are actually doing: that they are cutting covenant with the other party in the presence of God, His angels and the human witnesses. That's why all those people are there on your marriage, to bear witness of the covenant that you are cutting with your spouse. It is powerful and serious. You used the words you uttered to the other party to commit yourself, and sealed it with the ring. The witnesses are asked if anyone has a reason that should stop the proceeding. Nobody usually talks that this man is too violent; he killed his first wife; this woman is a robber, she robbed a bank ...everyone keeps quiet until the covenant is completed. Then the minister continues by saying that if no one has anything to say to stop this marriage proceeding, let every mouth be silent forever concerning them in Jesus name, the Church responds: "Amen" meaning, let it be so.

Every word of the marriage covenant, by the word of God spoken at that altar of God (where the presence of God also dwells), is written down in God's book. As soon as the minister pronounces you husband and wife (not man and woman), Heaven also pronounces you husband and wife. The woman's name automatically changes to the man's name. The minister says: you may kiss the bride – that is, open romance before everyone present. Then the minister will speak on the word of God that says: For this cause shall the man leave his father and mother and cleave to his wife and the two shall be one flesh: what God has joined together, let no one put asunder.

The covenant of marriage continues with the consummation of the marriage. The consummation of marriage refers to the sexual union and the co-habitation of the couple. Here sex is holy, undefiled and blessed. Marriage has been consummated. If the woman was a virgin, which is necessary, her first sexual experience will require the breaking of her hymen, which will produce blood from her. God put that hymen there for a reason. Some interpretation says that the consummation of the marriage union which results in the breaking of the hymen (if there is any) and causes the blood to flow is a symbol of the final consummation of the marriage covenant. Whatever is the case, the sexual union is a symbol of their covenant of oneness which in turn will produce godly seed in that marriage – that is the purpose of God. It is holy, blessed and good in the sight of God.

The oneness between a man and his wife is spiritually

embedded. They are no more two, but one. In this union, the two are made one inside Christ. As long as they stay in Christ, He will continue to hold them together in love, peace, unity and daily creating new things in them and through them. We shall look more into this symbol of marital unity, later.

Chapter 4

CHRIST AND THE CHURCH: THE SYMBOL OF MARRIAGE COVENANT

It was he who gave some to be apostles, some to be prophets, some to be evangelists, and some to be pastors and teachers, to prepare God's people for works of service, so that the body of Christ may be built up until we all reach unity in the faith and in the knowledge of the Son of God and become mature, attaining to the whole measure of the fullness of Christ. (Ephesians 4:11-13).

The relationship between Christ and the Church is unity and full measure of the unity of the Church with Christ. The Bible says that all have sinned and fallen short of the glory of the LORD. The original purpose of God in creating man was broken. Man was separated from God. So through the death of the LORD Jesus Christ, and the shedding of His Blood, His Blood became the sacrifice needed to purchase us back to God and to restore man back to glory. So through His Blood, we are purchased unto God, and we are united with Christ as one in Him.

He betrothed us unto Himself as our Husband, and we are His Bride. He became our strength, our joy, our life, our inheritance. His glory is our glory, His kingship our kingship, and His Priesthood, our priesthood. We are therefore, called a royal priesthood because of our marriage marriage to the King of Kings and the High Priest of the

Most High. As the Bride of Christ we partake of His oneness, being made conformable unto His image until we come to full maturity in union with Him and the Father. Right now, we are betrothed to Him:

> *I will betroth you to me forever; I will betroth you in righteousness and justice, in steadfast love and mercy. I will betroth you to me in faithfulness, and you shall know the LORD. (Hosea 2:19-20).*

> *I am jealous for you with a godly jealousy. I promised you to one husband, to Christ, so that I might present you as a pure virgin to him (2 Corinthians 11:2)*

From the Old Testament to the New Testament, we see instances where God referred to His relationship with His people as marriage. In the Old Testament, He pledged His love, His faithfulness and mercy to His betrothed, His people to whom He was married.

Whenever His people however, began to worship foreign gods, He addressed it as harlotry, and He had to woo them back in compassion renewing His marital faithfulness to them. In Jeremiah 3: 14 He says to His wayward people:

> *Return, O backsliding children, saith the LORD; for I am married unto you: and I will take you one of a city, and two of a family, and I will bring you to Zion.*

> *Not according to the covenant that I made with their fathers in the day that I took them by the hand to bring them out of the land of Egypt; which my covenant they brake,*

although I was an husband unto them, saith the LORD: (Jeremiah 31:32 (KJV)

And I saw, when for all the causes whereby backsliding Israel committed adultery I had put her away, and given her a bill of divorce; yet her treacherous sister Judah feared not, but went and played the harlot also (Jeremiah 3:8)

Also in Isaiah 54:5, He called Himself Husband to His people: ...*for your maker is your Husband*. In some other place, in comforting His people concerning their regathering again as a nation during the Millennium reign of Christ, He pledge to marry them again:

You will be a crown of splendor in the LORD's hand, a royal diadem in the hand of your God. No longer will they call you Deserted, or name your land desolate. But you will be called Hephzibah, and your land Beulah [which means married], for the LORD will take delight in you, and your land will be married. As a young man marries a maiden, so will your sons marry you; as a bridegroom rejoices over his bride, so will your God rejoice over you. (Isaiah 62:3-5).

He entered into the covenant of marriage with His people Israel when He redeemed them from Egyptian bondage and brought them into Mount Sinai where, through Moses He gave them His word: His Laws and statutes and they covenanted to live by His word:

*And Moses took half of the blood, and put it in basons; and half of the blood he sprinkled on the altar. **And he took the book of the covenant, and read in the audience of the people: and they said, All that the LORD hath said will we do, and be obedient. And Moses took the blood, and sprinkled it on the people, and said, Behold the blood of the covenant, which the LORD hath made with you concerning all these words** (Exodus 24:6-8)*

When He divorced His people due to their unrepentant waywardness, He gave His Son to shed His Blood as a covenant of peace with His people. And now, He has redeemed (purchased) us, the Church through His Blood unto Himself, and became our Husband. What the LORD Jesus is to the Church (a Husband), is what a husband is to the wife. Just as Boaz had to redeem Ruth, the widow of the dead son of Naomi and brought her into his wealthy place as his wife, so Christ our Kinsman- Redeemer has married us unto our God, into His royalty, His Priesthood, his Kingship, unto God. We are His Bride to share in His inheritance and share in His eternal life with the Father. We are one in Him (John 17: 23). In Ephesians 5:25-27; 32 the husbands are encouraged to love their wives as Christ loved the Church and gave Himself for her:

Husbands, love your wives, just as Christ loved the church and gave himself up for her to make her holy, cleansing her by the washing with water through the word, and to present her to himself as a radiant church, without stain or wrinkle or any other blemish, but holy and blameless. This is a profound mystery— but I am talking about Christ and the church (Ephesians 5:32)

Christ loves us so much that He took the place of the punishment of the world to the Cross and died the accursed death: death by hanging on the Cross. He stood condemned on behalf of the world, and rose from the dead on the third by the power of the Holy Spirit, setting us free from the powers of Satan and Hell. He carried our diseases upon His Own Body on the Cross so that through His stripes we have been healed. Christ did all these for us because we, the Church cannot do them. He redeemed us out of the world, sin, sickness, nakedness and covered us with his righteousness, strength, purity, holiness and through the Holy Spirit continues to teach and lead us until we become and are conformed to His image- the very image in which God made us. One day, He will come for His bride (the Church). He is continually preparing us, interceding for us and getting us ready for the final consummation of His bride: The Church: *Hallelujah! For our LORD God Almighty reigns. Let us rejoice and be glad and give him glory! For the wedding of the Lamb has come, and his bride has made herself ready. Fine linen, bright and clean, was given her to wear* (Revelations 19:6-8).

Fine linen represents the righteousness of Christ; which Christ gave His Bride (the Church) to wear. This gives us right standing before God, the Father Who is of purer eyes than to behold iniquity. We are therefore, free from condemnation; we are faultless and blameless before God. It is Christ that took all these pains to make His Bride - the Church, ready for the final consummation of the marriage, which is the rapture of the saints and present us before the Father. It is love that compels Christ to make all these sacrifices for his Bride the Church and continues to make us.

In the same way, the man is asked to love his wife just as Christ loved the Church and gave himself for her. The love of Christ causes Him to continue to purify the Church with his Blood and the water of His word, continually making intercessions for her and ministering to her by the Holy Spirit and the angels –all in order to present to Himself a chaste and holy people without spot and wrinkles unto the Father.

What Christ is to the Church is what a husband is to his wife. During the marriage covenant, he commits himself through his words to cherish, love, adore, support her and provide for her. He is also to emotionally and physically support and protect her by taking it upon himself to keep her and to protect her from harm. His sacrificial love will cause the wife to love, respect and submit to him. I am not saying that except a woman convinces herself that her husband loves her, she will not submit, no not at all. I am saying, by the word of God that your selfless commitment to her will release great respect and honor from her to you. In 1 John 4: 19, it is written that we love Him because He first loved us.

God knows that when a man commits himself in sacrificial love to his wife as Christ loved the Church that such a wife will respond to it. Today, many people endure hardship, agonies even unto death in demonstrating their love for Christ in serving Him. We so much appreciate His sacrifice on the cross on our behalf, redeeming us from the bondage of sin, curses, poverty and ultimate punishment in Hell that most people are willing to give Him all to reach out to the poor, the needy and the lost souls with the message of the cross. A husband's love and heartfelt commitment to his wife will therefore, produce a great action of love and submissiveness in his wife (the wise woman). So the union of husband and the wife is the symbolic union of Christ and the Church, and it is only through the Blood of Christ, and in Christ that marriage union can be sustained.

CONSEQUENCES OF BREAKING GOD'S COVENANT OF MARRIAGE

As long as the Body of Christ, the Bride of Christ, stays under the covenant of love and unity with Christ, obeying His word and doing the will of God, they have Christ's protection, provision and coverage. They have all the benefits of the covenant: the Abraham's covenant blessings which He purchased for us through His Blood; they also have the love of God demonstrated to us through the LORD Jesus on the Cross and they have the entire treasures of Heaven laid out for them. But if the Bride (the Church or any of His own) leaves the Bridegroom (Christ), she is out of divine protection and coverage and is exposed to the ravaging wild beasts –Satan and his agents. Most people die instantly or have their last state worse than the beginning because; the enemy goes back with seven more deadly demons to get the person into greater bondage. In the same way, when the couple or any of the couples begin to willingly walk away from God's covenant of marriage through abuses or disobedience to the word of God, if the problem is with the husband who is the head of the home, there is problem with the entire body, the family. The husband or whoever has broken the covenant will begin to walk in the deceptions of the enemy:

> *And with all deceivableness of unrighteousness in them that perish; because they received not the love of the*

truth, that they might be saved. And for this cause God shall send them strong delusion, that they should believe a lie: That they all might be damned who believed not the truth, but had pleasure in unrighteousness. (2 Thessalonians 2: 10-12KJV).

The above verse is self-explanatory. The person, who knows or understands the truth (the word), but refuses to love and embrace that truth, but begins to walk in the deceitfulness of the way he has chosen for himself, in unrighteousness, God will send to such a person a strong delusion to believe lie (to believe what is false). This will cause such a person to perish. We see that in marriage therefore, as one of the couple begins to depart from the marriage covenant and refuses to allow the word of God to correct him so that he can return to his marital responsibilities, he is heading for destruction. In such a case, marriage becomes struggles and full of arguments and strife. It is written that where there is strife, there is confusion and every evil work (James 3:16). With strife and so forth, things begin to fall apart in the family. The enemy begins to have a field day in their marriage, while the children's lives begin to fall apart as they try to find security and stability, which home is no longer giving them, outside.

Breaking the covenant, which you made before God is very consequential. Many people have died in the process or hurt themselves in various ways. After committing themselves in marriage covenant, some people begin to take the word of the covenant for granted. Consequentially, numerous problems begin to erupt as described above. At last, the marriage ends up in divorce or separation, while some people end up dead. Some things that cause the breaking of covenant shall be discussed in the next chapter.

NOT LEAVING, NOT CLEAVING

Therefore, shall a man leave his father and his mother, and shall cleave unto his wife: and they shall be one flesh. And they were both naked, the man and his wife, and were not ashamed (Genesis 2: 24-25).

This is a controversial issue in many families that even some of the very elects have used it to oppress their own marriages. God is God and not man. Some people that even call themselves marriage counselors have twisted this message to satisfy the desires of the male counterpart, who would not let go of his people in marriage. At times, some people say it in such a way as though the woman or the man (depending on who is the victim here) wrote that scripture and so; they use it to intimidate her. She ends up becoming a house-help in her marriage because; she is married to her husband's entire family and must accommodate them all in her marriage: serve them all so they will accept her as "our wife".

This is more prevalent in African tradition. She is not to complain because, they would not want her to be seen as coming to destroy the unity that holds her husband and his people, so she continues to live under the hard pressure and oppression of her husband's people. She has lost her identity. And because, the foundation of that marriage is not being laid in Christ but on tradition, too many evils will start happening on it. In most cases, the in-laws will send her away because she is not a good wife (of course she won't be) as she could not please everyone. She is miserable.

In some cases, to cope with such a situation, some of such women become manipulative or bitter. In manipulation, she would treat her husband's people good in his presence and bad in his absence. She is scheming and manipulative, because she does not want to lose her marriage, and not wanting her husband to see her as a bad person to his people. This is one of the perils of tradition in marriage. Check out my oncoming book: Traditional conflict in marriage. When God ordained marriage, He established the above law/foundation: For this cause shall a man leave his father and his mother and cleave to his wife and the two shall be one flesh. It is the foundation of marriage. If a man will not leave his people, he cannot and will not cleave to his wife. The old wine skin will have to go for the new wine to take place. Old life will have to go for the new life to take place. So old attachments, unity with your people will have to go for you to form one union with your wife. I did not write it, God did. The LORD Jesus says that He brought a sword in the world, a mother-in-law against her daughter-in-law (Mathew 10: 35). What this means is that, for the word of God to take place in your life, in your family, something there will give way. The word of God is the sword that puts asunder the old from the new. The mother has to let her son, go. Psalm 45: 10 says: Forget also your own people, your father's house, for the King delights in you. This scripture as well as applies to our relationship with our LORD Jesus Christ, it also applies to marriage union. In both relationships "cleaving" takes place after "leaving".

You say: "I cannot leave my son to that bitch; that witch. She has bewitched my son. I will make sure I will control the situation so she will not steal my son from me".

Well, that is why you should have spent so much time in prayers and even in fasting, covering your son spiritually until the LORD directs the right person to him. When a godly woman enters into the life of your son and you allow the word of God to take place in that marriage, your daughter-in-law and your son will marry you like a wife. This is because, you did not go fighting your daughter-in-law over your son, but you humbled yourself to God and continue to uphold them in prayers, with godly wisdom and counseling so their foundation would solidly be laid on the word of God. You want grand-children that will be healthy, happy, and loving you. You want to be part of their lives for good: then give place to the word of God. If Naomi was a bad mother-in-law, Ruth would not have chosen to leave her people and everything behind to go with her, when she did not even have any hope of getting into marriage with anyone else. She cleaved to her godly mother- in-law, a woman full of faith who extolled the word of God above anything else. She was a loving mother and a role model to Ruth and so, Ruth cleaved to her assuring her that her God would be her God, and her people would become her people: only death could separate them from each other. She was literally giving her life over to this woman. She never thought of her comforts anymore. What did she see? It was the love that Naomi radiated through her faith in God. Their commitment to the word of God and to each other made them heroes of faith and the genealogy of the LORD Jesus Christ. God saw their unity and oneness of purpose in Him. He saw their faith in Him through His word and blessed Ruth with the wealthiest man in the land, who loved her so much and willingly redeemed her through marriage. God honored Naomi's faith and gave her a grandson, Obed who was the father of Jesse, David's father. Our LORD Jesus Christ descended from this lineage. Jesus Christ is called the Son of David.

During a marriage ceremony between a husband and his wife, they vow to leave everyone else to cleave to each other. This is because; the word of God says so. When a man accepts his wife as his wife; loves and cherishes her as one flesh with him, honoring the covenant he cut with her in the presence of God, His angels and human witnesses, no one can come between them. That will offend his people, but it is the responsibility of the man to sit down with his people with love and understanding and explain to them that as a married man, his priority is his family-his wife. Though he will still help to take care of them, but his life, his decision-making will be with his wife. As he does this and stands by his word, his people will respect his choice. Whenever they attack his wife, he stands to protect her and not accuse her of coming between him and his people. As his people continue to notice that attacking his wife will even estrange their son/brother from them, they will submit to the principles that guide that marriage and respect them as a family.

DANGERS OF NOT CLEAVING

When a man is not submissive to the word of God that asks him to leave his people and cleave to his wife, he opens himself up to something else to cleave, and as mentioned above, he begins to live lie. Since he is not cleaving to his wife, his heart is not with her. That's when God calls his people harlots. God is married to His people and He wants them to love Him with all their hearts, soul and all their might. But when the people of God begin to have another priority apart from God, and set their hearts onto it instead of God, if it is job, at times God causes them to lose it so they would return to their first love-loving and serving Him with all their hearts and might. In the Old Testament, when they began to worship foreign gods, after warning them for some time, He caused them to be uprooted from their land or handed them over to an oppressor so that they would eventually repent and return to Him because, He is married to His people and is jealous over them. In the same way, when a man is not cleaving to his wife, he becomes wayward in the sense that his heart will begin to wander on something that will take the place of his wife in him. He may return and attach himself to his people, in such a circumstance he is not married to his wife but to his people. He could also start looking for an affair outside because; something has to take the place of his wife to whom he would not commit himself. Something else also could still take him away, but he will surely be committed to something. The situation also affects some ministers of God, who are married to the ministry and their ministry partners at the expense of their marriages. Just as God always woos us back, He through the Holy Spirit constantly speaks to the man to return to his wife. Most men would not because of fear of what people might think of them.

If the man continues to reject the word of God to cleave to his wife, and refuses to be committed to her, they are not one flesh anymore, and he will never see her as his wife, but his enemy. He will start criticizing her for one thing or another. Such a marriage is no longer heading to the right direction. Refer to the explanation on the previous chapter. That's why many marriages are full of violence. A man belittles his wife, beats her up, disgraces her, and deprives her of her needs because; he does not have respect for her. He is not in unity with her. He does not cherish her. He considers her sub-standard to him. He has embraced lie rather than truth because he refuses to love and embrace the truth, the word that the LORD God set out for the success of their union. It is written: For I say, through the grace given unto me, to every man that is among you, not to think of himself more highly than he ought to think; but to think soberly, according as God hath dealt to every man the measure of faith (Romans 12: 3). A man is not to think that he is better than his wife for both the man and the woman are equal joint heirs of the manifold grace of God.

This situation also could be vice versa. She could also be a carrier woman who spends all her time in her carrier, or works many shifts in her job to the neglect of her husband. She could also be an abuser, controlling and manipulating her husband, enslaving him. It could be a woman that could not leave her people and so she carried her family into her marriage. When the couple forsakes the word of God and begins to live in rebellion, which is witchcraft, the presence of God leaves the marriage and the enemy enters. It will take God's intervention to save such a marriage. The offending spouse or the stubborn one needs to submit to the counsel of the Holy Spirit, to return to the vows he/she made at the altar of God, in the presence of both the Heavenly and Earthly witnesses, to love and embrace the word of God for their family so that God can heal them. Nothing is impossible with God.

When I got married, I went to Lagos to start waiting to acquire visa to travel. I began to remember my people especially those of them that were crying that day as I was being handed over traditionally, to my husband's people. I could not stop thinking about them. I cried and cried and started thinking of going to visit them. The Holy Spirit said to me that I was married and I was asked to leave my people physically, mentally, psychologically. I needed to detach myself from them and face where I was going. I really thought that scripture was only meant for men until the LORD cautioned me with it. So it is meant for women, too. I know of a lady in my area whose mother controlled her so much in her marriage to the point that even her children were transferred to her father's house. Her husband did not have a good job, but she was doing well. So, she and her husband began to cook on different pots. There was no peace at all. Her mother was in control of her life, finances and all. The Church elders tried to intervene, but that did not help as at the time I knew about the situation. I believe that the marriage did not survive since the woman was living in deception. The influence of in-laws is one of the reasons why some people cannot cleave in the marriage. Psalm 45: 10, *Listen, O, daughter, Consider and incline your ear; Forget your own people also, and your father's house; so the king will greatly desire your beauty.*

Whenever God specially calls someone, He demands ultimate separation from the past. He called Abraham and asked him to leave his people, his father's house and follow Him to the land He was going to show him. Abraham however, left with Lot. It was not until he completely severed from Lot that the LORD confirmed His covenant with him. Also, in Esther's preparation for marriage to the King, she was prepared with the oil of myrrh and some other spices for twelve months. Myrrh means bitter. This is a purification process which involves dying to oneself in order to be made ready for the King (Esther 2: 3; 6: 13). She had to let go her past and embrace the bitter preparation of self-denial in marriage to the King. Without going through the bitter suffering of this preparation with the oil of myrrh, which produces sweet aroma (to the King), she would not be ready to become the King's bride. Since our relationship with the LORD Jesus Christ is marriage, we let the Holy Spirit prepare us with this oil of myrrh as we daily crucify our fleshly desires and embrace the cross, allowing Him to prepare us through trials of our faith to produce in us the precious characters of the Holy Spirit, which include: patience, endurance, longsuffering. These are the characters of Christ, which make us a sweet smelling savor of Christ before God, our Father. The word of God compares our marriage with Christ with earthly marriage. The couple therefore, is asked to leave the old; allow the Holy Spirit to prepare you with the bitter oil of self-crucifixion as you let go of the past and cleave to each other in love so the LORD will radiate His glory through your union, and also to use your union to help fulfill His great plan for mankind. Marriage is therefore, a commitment from the two parties both physically and prayerfully.

From what we said above, unless your marriage is rooted on the foundation of Christ, the Rock that God placed it, the foundation "you build it" will get rotten and the marriage will decay. The word of God says that other foundation shall no man lay except that which God has already laid. It is the foolish man that builds his house on the sand instead of the Rock-the word of God. Such a house according to the word of God cannot survive the pressures and storms of life.

Chapter 5

REASONS FOR NOT CLEAVING

WRONG COUNSELING AND TEACHING

This may seem light, but wrong teaching is evil. In Revelation 2: 20-23,

> *Nevertheless, I have this against you: You tolerate that woman Jezebel, who calls herself a prophetess. By her teaching she misleads my servants into sexual immorality and the eating of food sacrificed to idols. I have given her time to repent of her immorality, but she is unwilling. So I will cast her on a bed of suffering, and I will make those who commit adultery with her suffer intensely, unless they repent of her ways. I will strike her children dead. Then all the churches will know that I am he who searches hearts and minds, and I will repay each of you according to your deeds.*

Some people do take half of the word of God and mix it up with their own understanding explaining that the word of God did not mean what it says. From the above prophesy to the Church of Pergamum, the LORD Jesus warns against the danger of eating food meant for idols. The food meant for idols are the mixing of the word of God, and one's ideas (or pagan ideas) for evil purpose or to accomplish some selfish or satanic purpose. It is not a light thing because the word of God warns us not to add or to remove from the Word of God (Proverbs 30: 6; Revelation 22: 18-19; Deuteronomy 4:2, 12:32). No prophecy of the scripture is of private interpretation (2 Peter 1: 20). I have taken time to make these references because, it is absolutely important that we do not interpret the word of God in our understanding thereby adding or subtracting. It is consequential. Many people have been deceived by false prophets who add and subtracts from the word of God, and who also gave them wrong prophetic directions. I always warn parents to be careful who teaches their children in Children Department of their local Churches and also to pay attention to what they teach them. At times, they ought to go and stay with them in that department because, agents of Satan often work in the House of God as ministers, indoctrinating people especially children and the youth into wrong doctrines. In *He came to Set the Captives Free* by Rebecca Brown, she emphasized this truth through Elaine. Elaine, one of the top witches in the USA before she surrendered her life to the LORD Jesus Christ, confessed that she led youth ministries. In the process of leading the youth, she recruited many of them into Satan's Kingdom and also taught them half-truths and half lies. As a child of God now, she regrets how much time of those youth she wasted indoctrinating them on wrong teachings.

This same thing is also applied to some counseling by marriage counselors. If you are genuinely a counselor and working for God in this sensitive area or any other area, please pray over matters before giving out your counsel because, there is power in words. Your counsel may do or undo families, lives and people concerned. Do not interpret any scripture to suit one of the couple you want to please, because no scripture is of any private interpretation. "For do I now persuade men, or God? Or do I seek to please men? For if I yet pleased men, I should not be the servant of Christ" (Galatians 1:10, KJV). You are either doing the will of God through your counseling, or the will of the enemy. If a counselor leads someone out of the word, the person will surely embrace falsehood and damnation.

Many people are living misguided lives in their marriages through wrong counseling. Other foundation shall no man lay except that which was laid...the LORD Jesus Christ, the eternal word of God. Most of such people already know and understand divine principles for marriage, but they would not embrace it. They rather seek such counselors that counsel them on what they want to hear, and so they embrace falsehood just as we described in the previous chapter (Refer to 2 Thessalonians 2: 10-12). Let's read it again:

> *And with all deceivableness of unrighteousness in them that perish; because they received not the love of the truth, that they might be saved. And for this cause God shall send them strong delusion, that they should believe a lie: That they all might be damned who believed not the truth, but had pleasure in unrighteousness.*

Such people who know the truth, but rather than embracing the truth of the word of God, they seek for counselors that will teach them what they must do according to their own lusts, God sends to such people spirit of error to believe lie

(Also, refer to Ezekiel 14:4).

King Ahab did not love true words from God from the mouth of Prophet Micah. God sent a lying spirit in all the prophets (four hundred of them), who were prophesying to him. It was the will of God to have him misled, to fulfill His word through Elijah, and to avenge the blood of his prophets and that of Naboth the Jezreelite, upon him. They all prophesied what he wanted to hear, except Micah, who prophesied the truth. Micah even revealed to him that the LORD God sent a lying spirit into the mouth of all those prophets who were prophesying to him. The LORD said:

> 'Who shall persuade Ahab, that he may go up and fall at Ramoth-gilead?'...And there came forth a spirit, and stood before the LORD, and said, I will persuade him. And the LORD said unto him, Wherewith? And he said, I will go forth, and I will be a lying spirit in the mouth of all his prophets. And he said, Thou shalt persuade him, and prevail also: go forth and do so. (1 Kings 22: 20-22).

In spite of this revelation from the true prophet Micah, King Ahab rejected this true prophecy but rather chose to embrace lie that he would prosper in the war and come back in peace, just as those false prophets prophesied to him. He sent Micah to prison for prophesying true words from the LORD, and went to the war. He died in that war. This is the same reason why many people live in falsehood, and would not see any reason to take the right decision. They continue to justify their wrong mindsets which they have adopted. Ignoring the Voice of God, they accepted the voice of the stranger. They are heading downhill.

While discussing with a Pastor, a very zealous Pastor

about marriage one day, he made a reference as to what a marriage should be. He ignored anything that has to do with the word of God and began to try to educate me on the traditional mindset of marriage. This Pastor always mentioned to me that he was counseling couples. I began to wonder if that was the counseling he had been giving to couples. I will discuss more on this in the next line of thought.

In chapter two, I discussed how I was handed over to the in-laws who hated me. While the prophecy he received as a High School student might be true, we still needed to put things in proper order according to the word of God. Besides, the word of God warns us not to despise prophecy but to test all things. The word of God interprets itself. When a prophecy works contrary to the written word of God, then it's not from the LORD no matter how good it sounds. So in a bid to fulfil that prophecy and keep the tradition of their unity: no marriage, no children will stand on his way. So, he devoted all his resources for that one reason. The word of God says that if anyone does not provide for his household, his immediate household, he has denied the faith and is worse than an infidel. Our God is God of order, not of confusion. Our marriage never survived because he maintained a different mindset and walked on it. Our marriage, built on this false foundation could for as long as he continued to walk on falsehood, things continued to get worst each passing day, as there was no sure foundation on which to build. There was no commitment as that might interfere in their unity and plans for his people.

Jezebel was a prophetess, who killed the true Prophets of God. In Revelations 2:20, the LORD said that by her teachings, she misleads my servants into sexual immorality and the eating of food sacrificed to idols (mixing God's word with paganism/tradition).

However, Miracle and I suffered greatly during the period I mentioned earlier. She was denied milk and cereal, and I was denied any good food to produce healthy breast milk. Nothing I said could move my husband, because he had to do everything based on what his unity with his people planned or said. He never opposed any aspect of the unity no matter how often I tried to communicate our sufferings to him. Our sufferings therefore, continued till the first five months since I had the baby and had nothing to feed her or me. He later became convinced that we were starving, He sent us some money. This angered his people, and they beat me up, seized most of my belongings and threw us out to the streets. We became homeless. I survived by preaching the gospel in buses and hospitals, while trusting the LORD to supply our needs for daily bread and somewhere to lay our heads each night. I was seeking first His Kingdom, preaching the gospel in buses and hospitals and on the streets, while He took care of our basic needs. After seven and half months on this condition on the streets of Lagos with my baby, the LORD intervened for us with a miracle.

Before this, a widow who always saw me around Christian Pentecostal Mission Headquarters in Lagos said that she was unable to sleep each night she saw the baby and me, without being sure where we would sleep each night. She brought us into her apartment. There, the LORD put money into my hands, which I used to fix myself up and bought some baby foods for my baby. That week, the Sunday night after the end of the year's communion service in CPM, I hit the road awaiting a bus to the woman's house, but the Holy Spirit whispered into my ears to go to the airport (Murtala Muhammad International airport, Lagos) and see if my husband was back. It is just a bus-ride from the Church bus-stop. Suddenly, I felt a light moving towards that direction. I went straight to the airport, and into to the British airline office. He used to travel on that airline. He was on board. I did not know he was coming home that day. That was how the LORD united us again for that period. This also fulfilled the LORD's promise to me that: The hands of Zerubbabel have laid the foundation of this house; his hands shall also finish it (Zachariah 4: 9). By this intervention, God destroyed all the plans of new wife they planned to give him as soon as he arrives into the country and gets to the village. It was such a great miracle that proves the omnipotence and faithfulness of God to those who put their trust in Him. We still fought and won more battles for the next two years until we travelled to be with him in the US.

One of the troubles many marriages also suffer is when men began to compare or expect their wives to be like someone else, who is considered successful. Don't wish your wife to be someone else. It is written that they are not wise that compare self with self. Don't desire to have your wife be like another woman because, you don't know how the other woman got to where she is. Besides, she is a different person with different virtues and talents, and also with different calling. Allow your wife to be herself in your life and develop her God-given potentials. Besides, it is not wise to try to get an input from another woman concerning your wife. She may not like your wife, or is envious of her and so, might set you up against her. I watched a movie where a man was wrongly suspecting his wife of infidelity, but the woman with whom he was talking continued to set him up against his wife until he beat his pregnant wife into coma and she died. Don't listen to another woman's ungodly inputs concerning your wife. The counsel of the ungodly shall surely perish. Understand that God put certain graces in your wife to enable her help-meet you, as your wife, which no other woman has, including the one you think could be better. When you spark the little smoke you saw in her, you will see the fire come up and begin to enlarge. Your wife is the good thing in your life and the favor of God upon you.

On a general note, no matter how spiritual someone is or how much the person can prophesy to you, laying hands on the sick and they are healed, performing signs and wonders; whenever such a person speaks anything that is not in harmony with the word of God, reject everything and flee from the person. Such a person is destructive. If you don't flee from him/her, it is written in Proverbs 13: 20 that the companion of fools shall be destroyed. In Isaiah 8: 20, it is written that if they speak not according to this word, it is because there is no light in them. Do not be enticed with miracles and accurate prophecies and predictions, but be moved only by the word of God. I have written a book on how to identify and avoid false prophets and apostles. The book is titled: *The Church, the Bride of Christ: The True and the False Church (yet to be published).*

Meanwhile, don't open yourself up to people to speak into your life and family through counseling or anything. Some people want to get involved, not for your good; but to control the situations of your life especially if you are found "lucky" or blessed. Work out your salvation with fear and trembling. If the word of God you read cannot save your situation, counseling from anyone cannot unless you are directed by the Holy Spirit to go to such and such a person for help. Don't get too close to people when your marriage is in crises unless a prayer partner, who stands sincerely with you in prayers. Esteem the word of God above any advice or counseling. God gave us His Spirit as our companion to help, direct, counsel and guide us into all truths. The Bible talks about grievous wolves that entered into the body of Christ speaking perverse things and drawing men after themselves

(Acts 20:30). The Bible also speaks of tares among the wheat. They are hard to identify at the beginning, but you will know them by the fruit of their lips, their lifestyle or the effect of their words on you. Some of them are very manipulative and pervasive. Most of their words strike like arrows and will cause you not to sleep well at night. That is scorpion spirit. Each time they open their mouths, their very words want to suffocate their hearers. Their words are polluted words, because they don't flow from the spirit of life, they flow out of the abundance of their unclean hearts. Such words are also full of accusations and intimidation, which mostly ensnare the listeners. Such people are agents of Satan. You will know them by their fruits. When the very words of someone makes you feel little or unworthy, such a person is also an agent of Satan. He is operating by the spirit of witchcraft. He is robbing you of your worth through his/her words on you. Their counsels, the counsel of the ungodly shall perish whether they are Evangelists, Pastors, Prophets and all that. As long as their words disagree in part or completely with the word of God, flee from them.

The words that flow from the true counseling of the Holy Spirit are seasoned with salt, ministering grace to the hearers. Such counsels will edify and build you up, and are fruitful. The Bible says that the tongue of the righteous is a well of life; it is a river of life, not death. Before I open my mouth to speak in regards to marriage issues both in meetings and in open forums, when I listen to people paint matters, I simply lay it as it is written in the word. Why are people avoiding the word of God in marriages? Please allow the word of God to flow freely in your marriage. It is written that in Him we live, and move and have our being (Acts 17:28). He is the Head of all things, and He upholds all things including marriages by the power of His might. As long as a marriage therefore, is united in Christ, it needs to continue therein with the word of God and prayers to fulfill the purpose of God for it. There is a prophetic purpose for every family and it can only be fulfilled by submitting to the word of God.

TRDITIONAL INFLUENCE

What is regarded as tradition in Africa, maybe different in other parts of the world. Indians do arranged marriages for other reasons other than the word of God. In some other nations, such as Pakistan, some marriages are so arranged to the point that marrying someone other than the one that is arranged for the person could cause the woman's people to stone her to death. They call it, "honor killing", and the killer could redeem himself by paying "blood money", or they are simply forgiven. In such situation as traditional marriages, the people marrying each other are so much limited in their relationship with each other, as they have to fulfill the traditional expectations of their marriages. In some other parts of the world including here in the USA, tradition could mean a family expectation and norms whereby the husband and wife have to abide by the traditional norms and expectations, or face the consequences. Other parts of the world not mentioned here, have various traditions and expectations for a married couple.

African people have varied traditional norms with regards to marriage, even in naming a child. Some traditions are more powerful and more demanding than others. Here in America, I might not be able to identify exactly what tradition could mean in marriage, but I have seen or read few things. I once watched a (true life experience) movie whereby a woman who had sons had a tradition of being in charge of her sons' marriages. They had one kitchen, one cooking pot and everyone must submit to her: both her sons and all her daughters-in-law. One of the daughters-in-law rebelled, and pulled out from the community life she introduced. She plotted and killed her for her rebelliousness and independence. In such a situation, the tradition here is a family set up that a mother-in-law created to bring every one under her subjection, and her sons accepted it since they have no word of God to fight the situations. I have also seen another family where all the daughters must bring their husbands to live in one city. Every son-in-law must settle in the same city where others live, otherwise, the relationship is over. In these two examples, tradition is a family set up, which causes even the people involved to be limited in their marital choices. So then, tradition could mean different things to different people. In every way however, the believers in Christ are to abide on the Kingdom principles for marriage and not to follow the traditions of men. It is very surprising that even the Body of Christ in most cases embraces the traditional concept of marriage above the word of God. This makes it difficult for many couples in Christ to build their families on the foundation of the word of God, and if one of the couple tries to follow divine principles, if that is a woman, she is found to be a stubborn woman. This is mostly in third world countries. Paul asked: O foolish Galatians! Who has bewitched you … Having begun by the Spirit, are you now being perfected by the flesh? (Galatians 3: 1-3).

I spent all my childhood up to adult life studying and being taught the word of God. When I got married, I had only the word of God to bring into it. I gradually began to see and experience traditional conflict in marriages. Tradition is very antagonistic to marriage, and ultimately creates a very bad experience to couples. It is anti-marital happiness and health. Some men who are too attached to the tradition of their people cannot but try to bring in the tradition into their marriage. In spite of their exposure even to the word of God, they want the wife to naturally be the typical traditional wife that will do what is expected of her. She is seen as "wife" depending on how much she can handle well the traditional expectations of her. From my experience however, I discovered that tradition is rooted into Satan's kingdom. It has nothing to do with the word of God. It is paganism. It is witchcraft. My husband was expected to do many things God forbade His people from doing, and I always said no to him each time he mentioned any of such things to me. I continued to remind him that we as the people of God do not do such and such things. They continued to ask him to throw me out of the marriage.

The Church (the Body of Christ) is to carefully take this issue serious for somehow, it appears that tradition is mixed up with the word of God in most Churches. I believe however, that some churches, depending on the level of understanding and experience of the man of God, do pay attention to the perils of tradition. I remember the Church I attended and where we also wedded in Lagos, the Bishop emphasized on the need to cleave to one's wife. He spoke against traditional set up in marriages. So in such a Church, members that struggle with traditional problems can have it easily resolved with the godly counseling of such a Pastor. One of the ladies who wedded in that Church after me, briefly shared her experience of how both her and her husband were giving priorities to their in-laws, each struggling to make his/her people the priority. Then the man of God called two of them and warned them to make their marriage their priority, and never take decisions outside their union. The lady said to me that I was suffering because my husband was scared of what his people might think of him. I was sleeping in the empty Church's boys' quarter at the time, from where I was thrown out again. The Pastor, my Bishop at the time, hated the concept of "our wife" as in most African traditions, or bringing in your people to stay or share your home with the couple especially, when such in-laws pose threats to the wife. So in such a Church, the members would have good marital foundation and counseling with regards to traditional influence and live better married lives.

So many women however, are usually in trouble in their homes because of tradition. When my husband visited a year after our wedding, we learnt that a woman from their village was thrown out of her marital home, because she was not serving her husband's brother, who lived with them at the time. They specifically said that she was not washing his clothes. Within the same period in which I was there, another couple was also scattered. The man, a Pharmacist who met his wife in the University Campus and they were married, eventually returned to live in the village with their people. The complaint was that she was too wild for the in-laws. In the marriage where tradition has an upper hand, the woman will have to fulfill the traditional expectations of her, especially if she does not have the word of God to build her home. Those expectations however, are enslaving and deprive her of most of her marital rights especially if the man decides to bring his family to live together with the extended family.

Before my wedding, I waited upon the LORD for seven days through prayer and fasting. Then I had a revelation that had to do with: "Don't try to interfere in our unity", as I was always warned both by my husband and his people that they were/are in unity. I began to sense the perils of that. I remember clearly that I lost him to death in that dream, because of that tradition - his expectations which he always confessed to me that his people were his priority, (for a man of God prophesied that God would use him to establish them). I had settled that with me, since it was "a word of prophecy' over his life. I always said that to myself. But after the dream, I ran to the young medical student, who was spending time with the man of God in whose apartment we all lodged. I explained to him my dream and what fear that gripped my heart in this relationship because, I am not supposed to say or do anything or even see myself as should embrace him fully. This is because; he has tremendous responsibility towards his people. So, life was supposed to be him and his people. I was supposed to be a "wife" in the sense of third party. Despite everything I knew from the word of God, the fear that gripped my heart forbade me from getting too close or interfering in the relationship he said he had with his people. So the young student doctor picked up his Bible to read to me what is written concerning marriage; I said no, our marriage is different. I feel guilty to apply the word of God of "leaving to cleave" and besides, God might be making exception in my case because a man of God told him that God would use him for his people. In as much as this prophecy could be right or wrong, I don't think that the prophet would ask him to use the prophecy to destroy his family. Well, the marriage was all about his people. My mission probably (as I came to accept) was to come and help him establish, build and become deeply in unity with his people. The word of God was looking to me weaker than the strong pressure in me that said: "keep off, don't quote or apply the word here". It was such an intimidating situation. The young student doctor said to me that it is better to build marriage on the word of God than on the traditions of men. Besides, that love he has for his people, which is typical of African marriages, belongs to his wife and children. I was not listening to him. I was still scared to interfere. He began to fervently pray for me when he observed that what he was trying to explain to me was not getting to me. As he fervently prayed for me, I felt something like chain over my chest, brake. I have been delivered from that stronghold. Then I regained my confidence and had the boldness to stand firm on the word. A little later, another battle raged hard in my heart- "wicked person, selfish person; you want to own him all to yourself? That which is written in the Bible does not apply to your marriage…" I contacted another lady, a woman of God who had just taught me how to speak the word over all that concerns me and my marriage. She assured me that what I was experiencing meant that, that prayer hit the bull's eye and they were trying to bring me back under the bondage. However, with this new confidence whereby I began to build on the word of God; I continued to speak the word, exactly as it is written concerning marriage, meditating consistently and not giving up. Within few days of meditating and prophesying the word of God over my marriage, he wrote me that he was coming home for us to wed. The next month, like pulling something out of the mouth of the lion, that was how that wedding finally took place. The LORD thus asked us to wed where I worshipped at the time.

He came; we fought for the wedding - for the Church to let us wed. Eventually, the Church agreed to wed us on a Wednesday, and we wedded on the Saturday of the same week. Only the few that attended mid-week service knew about it. The Maid of Honor and the Best Man did not attend. Someone picked a beautiful gown and was my Maid of honor; and because we made a beautiful tuxedo suit already for whoever would be the Best Man, someone picked it up and was the Best Man. Back home however, all Hell broke loose. God asked us to wed in Lagos, but I was going to face a community of angry people whose son I wedded. According to him, his people wanted to stop the wedding, and refused to attend, but I only obeyed God and did as He asked me to do. You will pay highly for obeying the voice of God where tradition is deeply involved.

After he left, and I returned to the Church where we wedded, I met another sister, a member of our prayer team who just lost her family to the hands of her in-laws. They were living with her, created problems in the family and drove her away and took both the children and her husband. She was not good enough for their brother, and so she had to forfeit the children and her family. She was alone and was trying to figure out her new lonely life. In most cases, since there was no proper divorce, there is usually no marital property allocated to her to start her new lonely life over. I asked her if she did not know how to speak the word over her marriage, and stand on it -I mean the word of God that pertains to marriage-, she jokingly answered: "that is wickedness". To let the word of God have its free course in your marriage means that you will become your husband's wife and take charge of your family as yours, and not in-laws taking charge. Well, I continued to hold firmly the word of God that has to do with marriage, consistently speaking and meditating on them: These words include:

> My husband shall love me as Christ loved the Church and gave Himself for her...my husband and I are one flesh, we are naked together and are not ashamed; what God has joined together, no one shall put it asunder and on and on... (Ephesians 5: 25-26) My husband shall drink water only out of his cistern...he will rejoice with me the wife of his youth...and be ravished by my love. He will not be ravished by a stranger woman (Proverbs 5: 15-18).

However, it takes two to build a home. If the other person

is not in agreement with you concerning the word of God over marriage, it will become a very strenuous experience. When one person is heading to the East and the other, West; no matter how fast each of them runs towards their opposite destinations, there is no meeting point between the two. The Pastor of Grace of God Church, Bladensburg Maryland often said that. This is why it is good to wait upon the LORD for the right person, and if there are constant unresolved issues, communication problems, abuses, accusations, and lack of agreement concerning the implementation of the word of God or relating the marriage to the word of God, it is good to get off the hook before you say, "I do". I wrote more about this in the upcoming book: *Before You Get married.*

If you are a believer in Christ and in the tradition of unity with your people, you are under bondage. Allow the word of God to release you from such because, you are called to be one in Christ. You will eventually vomit the devil's gift. You are either on the LORD's side or you are not. The LORD Jesus said that those who are not for us are against us.

TRADITIONAL INFLUENCE IN THE BODY OF CHRIST

As a member of the Assemblies of God Church in Enugu, where I attended at the time with the in-laws, I began to have a great understanding of what is happening in the lives and marriages of some people of God. I understood how some people of God abandoned the Word of God concerning marriage over traditions of men. The word of God says that by tradition, they made void the word of God. When the High Priests and the Pharisees esteemed the traditions of men above the word of God, they began to oppress the people of God. The word was so void among them that they were working contrary to the principles of the very law they preached. They were teachers of the law which commanded them to love their neighbors as themselves, yet they saw a man beaten and robbed on the wayside, and passed by. They did not help him, until a Samaritan came and helped the dying man. They contended with Jesus for healing a blind man on the Sabbath day, and so forth.

Tradition violates the principles of the word of God, and imposes hard bondage on people. The Church women said things that marveled me, and made things worse for me. All their counsels were in favor of the in-laws' decisions, nothing from the word of God. They did not help me out even as I was starving with the baby, whereas my money was in the hands of the in-laws. All I was hearing was, since she refused to marry her brother-in-law first, let's see how she will go and marry her husband. This is not in alignment with the word of God. How many people are still going through this dilemma in their marriages in the House of God?

The Body of Christ is not to mix tradition of men with the word of God. Christ is the head of the home, and He is enough to handle the home. Recently, I was talking with the Pastor I mentioned earlier. He had just gone through a divorce and was trying to enter into another marriage. When I mentioned the situation about traditional influence in marriage, he said to me that no one would ever come between him and his mother. He enumerated everything his mother was to him, and said that a wise woman would always befriend the in-laws, and try to get her in-laws to love her so that her husband can love and accept her. I screamed out his name in that conversation and asked him if this is what he has been teaching the Body of Christ. He always counseled couples, was that the counseling he was giving out to people? Tradition above the word...feeding people with foods meant for idols? I already mentioned earlier that if your pastor, counselor and any minister gives you a counsel that is not completely based on the word of God, get away from such a person because, the counsel of the ungodly shall perish - whether they are pastors or prophets.

Such counsels always lead to destruction. The only sure foundation in marriage is the word of God. It is only a foolish man that builds his house upon the sand and such a house will crash down when storms and the waves of life come upon it (Mathew 7: 24-28). Tradition glorifies the works of the flesh which is enmity with God. Light and darkness cannot co-habit. Tradition, destroys marriages, enslaves the woman or man, whoever is the victim and negatively affects the lives of the children. I know many Churches pay attention to pre-marital counseling, which has helped young couples make right decisions to build their marriages on the right foundation, Christ. This is highly recommended in all Churches, because the young couples depend on what they learn from their spiritual authorities. The Bible encourages, the man to love his wife as Christ loved the Church and gave himself for her. The man is to protect his wife from the ravages of traditional set-up, but when he does that he will lose his reputation among his people, who would accuse him of being married to the woman. A woman who minds her business in her marriage with her husband and children is seen as a wicked woman; and the man that stands to cherish and protect her is seen as being influenced by his wife. So to please his people, many men find it difficult to cleave to their wives, because they would become less men in the eyes of their people. All that happens mainly, in African culture or third world nations where men dominate so much. When a man is not fully cleaving to his wife, he will take decisions without her knowledge. In her house, she is a piece of dirt before her husband and his people, because even the in-laws know that her husband does not discuss anything with her.

In some African families, a man who lives in the city and is considered wealthy sometimes tries to fill his house with his relatives. Sometimes, all the wife would see is someone move into her home without prior notice to her, except that the person had already discussed with her husband, who probably did not bother discussing it with her. In most cases, an in-law simply parks his or her things and moves into a couple's home without notifying both the man and his wife. Some women in such situations however, do not treat such in-laws or relatives well.

In such a typical African family where extended family system is given much preference, except the husband puts his foot down on behalf of his wife to get everyone treat her with respect, they will be finding faults with her, and there will be strife. If the husband did not put her in her marital position, she's always being seen with one weakness after another and will often be criticized because her husband does not show he values her. People see a woman from her husband's eyes. If she is a piece of dirt to him, that's how people will see her and talk to her. Her husband is her cover. So when the man fills his home with relatives, he is making his wife vulnerable and also creating an enmity between his wife and his people. If she does not want people living with her, but wants her privacy, that is okay for her. Then the man can make a different arrangement for his people somewhere else. As the joint owner of the home, she deserves the same honor that is being given to her husband. We are admonished to give honor to whom honor is due. She deserves the entire honor due her in her home.

The word of God encourages the man to leave his people to cleave to his wife. God showed me that a home belongs to the man, his wife and children. If someone else enters into the family unit, the person is bringing in a different spirit. The full unity is affected. So it is better, as I suggested earlier on that if possible, the man and his wife are to make a different arrangement for the in-laws they want to help in order to keep the family unit together. If a man never respects his wife's position and tramples on it, using the in-laws to humiliate and disrespect her, he will create a big enmity between his people and the wife. If for instance, anything happens to him, his family will be separated forever from his people, because they hated one another. His children will have nothing to do with his people. Again, the Holy Spirit is leading me to emphasize that the marriage belongs to the man and the woman with their children, only. They are to live together, alone. I will like to stop here on the issue of tradition and its influence on marriage, but I know so many learned, educated, well balanced ladies are trapped in this issue that's why I am boldly talking about it. I want to stop here on the issue of traditional influence on marriage.

EXTRA MARITAL AFFAIR

Extra marital affair is another reason why many couples are not cleaving to each other. Marriage, as we looked at it earlier on, is typical of the relationship between Christ and the Church. In His relationship with His people, God says that we are to love Him with all our hearts, soul and might. He wants deep intimacy with us, an unbroken union. He wants all of our being. When the LORD asked me to leave every job, business and everything and serve only Him, He knew that those things were distracting me from the total union He wanted from me. If an important man of God, who flows so much with the power and love of Christ to touch lives is divided in his union with God, he would not flow so much with the LORD's anointing/presence. God wants the world to see Him through us as we reflect His glory, His goodness, and the riches of His glory as He fully demonstrates Himself through us. His fullness can only be seen in our lives when we fully abandon ourselves to Him.

He asked Hosea to marry a woman named Gomer, a harlot. This would show His people what they were doing to Him in their waywardness in worshipping idols. That is what is happening to a marriage when a man claims he loves his wife and yet he is in love with other women. The word of God says that where your treasure is, is where your heart is. While extra-marital affair could mean sleeping with some other people apart from your wife or husband, it could also mean some other things. From God's description of His people's attitude of harloting under every tree, it was because His people's hearts were not with Him, but on other gods, whom they reverence and worship. In marriage, a man's heart is supposed to be first of all with God, then his family. God asks a man to love and cherish his wife. The reason God asks us for our hearts and also asks us to guard our hearts with diligence for out of it are the issues of life, is because as a man thinks in his heart so he is. If a married man is always thinking about another woman, that's where his heart is. It will eventually carry his feet to the bedchamber of that other woman. When your heart is always on someone else whether your mother, brother or another woman, that to me is extra-marital affair because that is where you will always be. That hinders you from cleaving to your wife. Also, when a man begins to sleep with another woman or have extra-marital affairs, he enters into a narrow pit. The Bible says that a strange woman is a narrow pit (Proverbs 23: 27). The reason the Bible calls her a narrow pit is because, when you enter into her, you will not come out again except by the grace of God. She is a trap. With one thing leading to another, she will eventually destroy your family or your life. Many great men lost their great status in life because of lust with a strange woman. One American President nearly lost his office as the president of America, because of a strange woman. David's troubles started when he lusted after another woman in his heart and had an affair with her. That sin led to many evils in his life including his almost loss of the throne to Absalom his son, who chased him out of the throne until God intervened for him. Many great men of God lost all they built for life with God, because of lust and affairs with other women. It is a deadly sin that pollutes the body and destroys the soul. It opens the door to demonic activities, because the sin of adultery is a one flesh union with the other party. The Bible says: *Know ye not that he which is joined to an harlot is one body? For two, saith he, shall be one flesh* (1 Corinthians 6: 16). It also opens doors for exchange of demons, which in turn will destroy the victim's family, even the children as those demons will begin to torment the entire family and relationships. I will talk more on this in one of my upcoming books: *Understanding and dealing with the foundational Pollution in homes*. It is dangerous beyond repair to engage and continue in extra-marital affair. It has caused too much heartbreaks and deaths to many couples and even caused many homes to break. One has to leave all that to cleave to one's wife so that they can become one flesh, indeed. Without cleaving, they are only sexual partners just like prostitutes, and eventually, because the foundation of that marriage is not good, it will eventually fall apart. It is written: *Don't be deceived, God is not mocked; whatever a man sows, that shall he reap* (Galatians 6: 7). What might seem to be a secret is not secret, because God knows about it. One day, after warning the person several times, He will expose him/her and great shall be the fall of such a person just like the house built on the sand. Also, because the word says that he who troubles his house shall inherit the wind; such a person might lose everything he/she built. Let it not be your portion.

When you cleave to your wife and forsake others just as you vowed, the presence and the glory of God will make you one indeed. You will experience the unity of oneness with the Father, Son and the Holy Spirit covered by His glory. You will experience great joy and blessings of God. Also, because you are naked together, hiding nothing from each other, you shall be helping each other from falling away. Remember you are joint heir together with the manifold grace of God. You are one in Christ. It is only in cleaving together that He can uphold your union with his power.

LACK OF COMMUNICATION

And they were both naked, the man and his wife, and were not ashamed (Genesis 2:25).

I briefly talked about this in Chapter two in regards to how communication affects sexual union. We will need to go further on this. The above verse speaks mainly of communication in marriage. It also talks about transparency in marriage. A couple is not to hide anything from each other. After the word of God says that the two shall be one flesh, it further states that they were both naked, the man and his wife, and were not ashamed (Genesis 2: 25). They let each other into their privacies. God knows that each and every one of His creation needs help - the support of one another. We need one another, that's why you cannot just

Jump into marriage just with anyone. In as much as there is no perfect person in the world, some people have teachable spirits and are willing to learn and grow together with you. They are open to adjustments and that is growth. Some people however, will never accept adjustments. In such situations, it is hard for the couple to communicate with each other, and make adjustments in areas where there is need for that.

In marriage, there is need for sacrifice. It is not a selfish relationship where the other dominates and wants the other to obey, submit: "don't tell me what your needs are, it is your entire fault". Many couples never, at any time, experience any type of communication breakthrough. It also happens in some ordinary friendship, but we are focusing on couples. In the course of writing this book, the LORD told me that a man never gets tired of listening to his wife. Christ died for the Church. We will look more on this later. You are to flow together. The Bible asks men to deal with their wives with knowledge, being of the same mind with the woman and submitting yourselves one to another. Let me say it again: submitting yourself one to another (Ephesians 5:21), and in 1 Peter 3: 7, it is written, *Likewise, ye husbands, dwell with them according to knowledge, giving honour unto the wife, as unto the weaker vessel, and as being heirs together of the grace of life; that your prayers be not hindered.* If you have the chance to talk about everything together, your spouse will know when something is going wrong and be able to handle it with you. Since you are of the same mind with each other, when you pray, the LORD will answer you. There is no limit to what you can achieve. The Bible says that one shall chase a thousand and two shall put ten thousand to flight. One, for one-thousand; but two, for ten-thousand. That is power of unity. Your unity in purpose, vision and agreement in the things that are right in the sight of God will cause you to become a sign and a wonder. It is written that when God saw that the people, who were building the Tower of Babel-the tower they meant to reach the heaven-were one, He said:

> *Behold, they are one people, and they all have the same language. And this is what they began to do, and now nothing which they purpose to do will be impossible for them. Go to, let us go down, and there confound their language, that they may not understand one another's speech (Genesis 11: 6-7).*

Even God would not be able to stop them because they were one, so God confused their language so that no one could understand the other, and scattered them abroad.

The way to destroy the unity between a husband and wife is communication problem. Whenever the couple sees any reason to hide information from each other, they start hardening themselves from each other, and would not want to cleave wholly to the other. Their marriage therefore is heading for destruction because hardness of heart will bring in anger, hatred and in some extreme cases, murder.

All of the above reasons I listed above as the reason why a man might not cleave to his wife, are also the same reasons for communication problem. Another major reason for communication problem and not cleaving together is materialism –love of money. Let's handle it as a chapter.

Chapter 6

LOVE OF MONEY, ROOT OF ALL EVIL

Here in America, and in some in some parts of the world, many marriages take place based on what you can bring into the union. Many African men came into America and adopted the pattern of life in the society. Most men marry women that will ease their financial struggles. In most cases, they marry Registered Nurses. As a matter of fact, many foreigners bring their wives here and make them do a nursing profession so they become Registered Nurses. This is because; it is believed that nurses work many shifts and could earn double income the same month.

In most cases in families, they become the head of the families, and switch God-ordained roles in marriage. The wife becomes the breadwinner, pay mortgages, build houses, sponsor the children in schools while the husband may take on cab driving or something that don't hassle him, a lot. On the other hand, many men are strongly providing for their families and their wives are also working too hard to provide for the family or to have a strong financial power. In some of such cases, the priority is money.

They may end up raising children through child cares, who will put into their children's lives what they have. When a child spends twelve hours a day in the hands of a total stranger starting from school in the morning till after school, and until six in the evening when the parents bring would bring him home, such a child is virtually raised by total strangers. The word of God encouraged the woman to be keeper at home. Make an arrangement to raise your children in the LORD, and to spend quality time with them each day so they can have the chance to learn a lot from you. Whatever is invested in their lives, whether from a total stranger or you, is what they will manifest in life. The Word of God says: Train a Child in the way he should go: and when he is old he shall not depart from it. The LORD Jesus told the following parable:

> *The kingdom of heaven is like a man who sowed good seed in his field; but while men slept, his enemy came and sowed tares among the wheat and went his way. But when the grain had sprouted and produced a crop, then the tares also appeared. So the servants of the owner came and said to him, 'Sir, did you not sow good seed in your field? How then does it have tares? 'He said to them, 'An enemy has done this (Mathew 13: 24-28).*

This happened because the parents are too busy chasing money at the expense of raising their children, even when God has already made enough provision in the home for the family. It is God that provides for the family, not your hard work. When couples put Him first and work according to His principles, they will discover that God surely takes care of families and brings promotion at the appropriate times. Don't try to be like others, that's when discontentment sets in.

God helped me take the right decision as I was having

my children, to stay home and raise them in spite of my cravings for job in their tender years. I went and obtained a diploma in Oracle database Administration, and was craving after how much I was going to make because; it was a very high income profession at the time, but the LORD kept holding me back. The birth of my second baby brought sudden promotion to my husband at work, and God had more plans to have us buy a good home. So in spite of all the income in the family, I was craving for personal income, and probably be like other women: drive nice car and be seen as a very hard working woman, as I always heard about others. Also, I wanted to do what was naturally expected of me, for my people, as one who is in the USA. I had just come up with my third baby; the second one who was barely eighteen months old had lost so much weight, but I was not paying close attention on why she was losing so much weight. She was not eating well, but it did not get my full attention as I was thinking of what I would be making in few months. One day, I was in a dream and was working too hard, struggling to make money. I heard a voice that asked in that dream: "What does … (my first and last name) say she wants?" I cooled a little bit after that voice, and got crazier, especially as I was watching many women make good money and live out their financial dreams. I was still two years old in the USA.

As I was completing my Diploma in Oracle DBA and planning to launch into the big time income job through the instructor who was collecting our resumes, the Holy Spirit spoke to me right in that class that I would not work with Oracle DBA, otherwise I would not write the books He wanted me to write. Obedience was not easy to come by to a woman who entered America and wanted to achieve financial independence. With the arrival of my third baby, I began to make arrangement for the job or another one, while planning to bring my mother to help care for her while I roll into job market. Again, I heard the Holy Spirit, ask me why I was craving after job instead of taking care of my children. When He asked me this question, it was as though I saw the flash of His face frown at my attitude of caring more for big income job, than for my children. Then, with a Voice laden with emotion He asked me: "don't you see how Esther looks?" I sat back and began to deeply feel remorse for my crave for the seeming high income job I believed I was about to land; and sorry for my baby, who had lost so much weight to the point that her butt was wrinkled and her hair falling. I tried her with various foods, but she could not respond, not even the doctor's advice could help. But now, I felt very sorry and began to focus on the situation to truly and fully care for my little girls. I laid the issue of job aside and began to do what the LORD said: be keeper at home. Immediately I took this decision, He gave me my first book to write: *How Do We Invest In Our Children?* Gradually, He started opening ministerial doors for me. Before I knew it, I was guest at some popular Radio stations and some Churches to minister in women programs, and so forth. We will look more into this on the chapter on Divine Role Play in Marriage. For more information on raising godly children, check my books: ***How Do We Invest In Our Children? and Raising Godly Children: Foundation Laid In Prayers***.

Meanwhile, continuing on the pursuit of materialism in marriage, when a marriage starts with the woman, who is considered to have a strong financial power, and the man relies on that, he probably loves her because of what she is bringing into the marriage. That marriage shall be likened to a house built on the sand. When a woman marries a man because of his profession and his financial power, that marriage is also a materialistic marriage. If God blesses you with a wealthy husband or wife, that is great. God's plan is for us to have abundant life in every area of our lives. However, we are not to take decisions based on what we see. Promotion comes neither from the east nor from the west, but from the LORD.

Materialism in marriage creates financial pressure and communication breakdown. The man would not want the wife to know about his secret investments and financial commitments. He is too busy to talk with her, because his job would not let him, or the wife is workaholic because she has to take care of financial responsibilities of the family, play the role of the wife and also be the mother of the children. And as she combines the male and the female roles together, she feels drained out, used and unappreciated. In some other cases, she wants to meet up a standard she has set up for herself (the peer pressure standard), trying to live up to-, and be like other women, with whom she competes

A woman, a Christian woman once asked me how much I was bringing into my marriage. Secondly, she asked why I chose not to be the one paying the house mortgage. She understood my commitment to my children, who at this time were in four different schools during summer, so that I was picking and dropping them to their various schools, help them with their homework and fully take care of them since they were still under age. I combined this with my Mary Kay business, and some other buying and selling businesses with which I had gotten myself involved. My husband at this time, was fully backed out of the family unit, always worked weekdays and weekends and was focusing only on his people back home. I was struggling like a single parent to raise four children on my own in the marriage. This (financially successful Christian) woman, who was said to go and advise me, concluded to me that if my husband was making $6,000.00 or thereabout in a month, she. would chose to make more than what he was making. They were circulating the news among themselves that I was not bringing in enough money into my family, and that was why I was going through marital crises. This group of women, most of them Registered Nurses, were their family breadwinners with their husbands bringing in little or nothing, but probably helping to care for their children. I was so much hated among them. In their advice to me to send all those children into daycare system and "go and work"; they never advised me on how to afford over $400.00/week in paying for daycare for them, be able to financially take care of their needs including feeding them, while looking for job. Besides, I was following divine instructions for my family, to forget about working outside the home, and raise my children by myself. To this end, I had to homeschool them at their early stage. Our obedience to God is often tried by fire.

Generally, however, in such a situation where a woman is determined to see to it that she makes more money than her husband for whatever reasons, at the expense of her children, there is some kind of competition in the marriage. The children might not be getting enough parental attention and nurturing, as the parents might have chosen an outsider to raise the children for them. Whenever materialism takes precedence in marriage, such a marriage often experiences communication problem which results to some other problems. There could not be adequate trust as one does not want the other to know how she/he spends the money being generated.

Some men who attained to a very high position and have great financial power before getting married see the wife as should be satisfied with all he provides for her. I have seen many women in marriages, who lack nothing materially in their marriages, but are the most heart-broken and miserable women. These women have the best cars, live in the best houses, and have beautifully well maintained children. They can purchase anything they need as long as money is concerned, but they are much unfulfilled. I once had the chance to sell some Mary Kay products (when I was a Director with the company) to one of them, who came to have a baby here in the USA. She was in a well-furnished rented condo, with her own car, and a cab-driver to attain to her personal needs, and surrounded with more than enough money. But her husband was busy with his job and business in different countries. If she felt lonely, she could go and shop as much as she needed. Back home, she would always see a Porsche or expensive cars driven in and the keys given to her, with dozens of suits for her to wear. She had so much that money could buy that she did not know what to do with all these material things. However, she needed her husband, which was the only thing missing in her life. The man that married her was always absent for weeks and months. Even as she had the baby, she was alone and needed him around, but he was not there. Each time she expressed her desire to have him around, the man would emphasize on the things with which he provided her and would still do more and more if that was what she needed. At times, such men mistake their wives need for them for sex.

These women or men, depending on who is always absent, need to understand that marriage is for companionship, not for money or sex, we discussed that earlier. Don't substitute your spouse's need of your presence for material things. In a marriage where materialism dominates, communication is lacking as we observed earlier, sexual intimacy is also lacking. Healthy communication produces healthy sex life in marriage. Materialism is not good in our relationship with God, as well as in marriage. Much unhappiness that abounds in many marriages is because; the other party considers the other too low for him or her, because he/she considers his material acquisitions as his, not theirs. That is why some couples sign pre-nup agreement before marriage so that each person keeps his/her wealth to him/herself. In case of divorce, there will no distribution of marital properties.

Many marriages suffer too much interferences, because many people especially relatives want to benefit from it, materially and the spouse is usually considered a potential threat to what they planned getting from them. In such a situation, the man or the woman needs to understand that your family is more important to you than material acquisitions or the people with whom to favor with those material things. Let the blessing of the material wealth be a blessing indeed to your family. Even when the man or the woman feels that the responsibility for the extended family rests on his/her shoulder; he is still to set his family as his priority. Let everything be done in agreement, understanding and love. Many men or women do intimidate their spouses always with "what I am today is so and so and so person", and they continue to emphasize on what they owe such a person. All things are to be done in prayers and with wise counsel even in assisting anyone materially. Such intimidating statements are not needed at all for the wellbeing of a marriage.

Also, if the pursuit of wealth is taking you away from your family, you need to seek the face of God for something that will work well for the family. Working many shifts to the point that the family could not benefit from the man or the woman's presence is usually detrimental to the marital unity. If one job is not giving you enough for the family, seek the face of the LORD for new open doors that will enable you to keep the family together and yet have more than enough for them. God is faithful and will surely provide more than enough to keep the family together. Many women have died here in America, because they are the bread winners for their family and as they work many shifts and earn too much, they at times become unavailable to the family. Most of them could become hot headed or felt unappreciated for all her hard works. Some of their men feel intimidated by the wife's success, or they feel they don't have enough respect from such women. Even if that may not be the case, where adequate communication exists in a marriage and each person plays his/her role well, things will work out well and the material acquisition becomes a blessing instead of a curse. We will see how to set the family in order in the next chapter.

Chapter 7

DIVINE ROLE-PLAY IN MARRIAGE

THE GODLY ROLE OF A HUSBAND

Husbands, love your wives, just as Christ also loved the church and gave Himself for her, that He might sanctify and cleanse her with the washing of water by the word, that He might present her to Himself a glorious church, not having spot or wrinkle or any such thing, but that she should be holy and without blemish. So husbands ought to love their own wives as their own bodies; he who loves his wife loves himself. For no one ever hated his own flesh, but nourishes and cherishes it, just as the LORD does the church. For we are members of His body, of His flesh and of His bones. "For this reason a man shall leave his father and mother and be joined to his wife, and the two shall become one flesh...Nevertheless let each one of you in particular so love his own wife as himself, and let the wife see that she respects her husband (Ephesians 5: 25- 33).

But if any provides not for his own, and especially for those of his own house, he has denied the faith, and is worse than an infidel (1 Timothy 5:8).

From the above verses, a man as the head of the home, is expected love, cherish and provide the necessary needs of his wife just as Christ loves, cherishes and provides for the Church. As the Holy Spirit woke me up one early morning, and began to give me some qualities of a father and a husband, I saw that God truly meant husbands to be like Christ in their relationship with their wives. My marriage was gone, and my husband left us for years now because of lack of commitment and abuses. As he left, some young men started approaching me for marriage. One early morning while still asleep, the Holy Spirit called me up and began to teach me some things about marriage...things I felt He wanted me to add to this book, and things to check out concerning any one proposing me for marriage. I picked up my pen and paper as He began to teach me what to expect from a father and a husband, and what not to expect.

A HUSBNAD NEVER GETS TIRED OF HIS WIFE

A husband never gets too tired to attend to his wife's need, or to listen to her. Christ loved the Church so much that He died for her. So no matter how tired a husband may be, he still needs to sacrificially pay attention to his wife's need or emotionally and physically support her just as Christ will never get tired of our prayers or tired of reaching out to us. In his *10 Men Christian Women Should Avoid*, Lee Grady listed the Narcissist as number 7. He says:

I sincerely hope you can find a guy who is handsome. But be careful: If your boyfriend spends six hours a day at the gym ...you have a problem. Do not fall for a self-absorbed guy. He might be cute, but a man who is infatuated with his appearance and his own needs will never be able to love you sacrificially, like Christ loves the Church (Eph. 5:25). The man who is always looking at himself in the mirror will never notice you (Lee Grady: 10 Men Christian women should never Marry, Charisma Magazine).

He is saying that a man that is too pre-occupied with himself is too self-centered, and will not have time to listen to his wife, or notice her needs. Most of such men have their personal schedules which hover around them each day. They don't let the wife in to their round-the-clock schedule that hovers around them. Some of such men could be engrossed with one business schedule after another...endlessly working. In their spare times, they have all planned out what they would do just for themselves. Most of such men are also into too much working out, spending tremendous amount of time each day in the gym and are too infatuated with their looks. Such self-centered men never find time to listen to, or hear what the wife is saying. They don't pay attention because they are not emotionally connected to her. Sometimes they joke over what she is trying to communicate, no matter how serious she is, or respond abstractly to her. It's not supposed to be so.

Many families including those of the men of God are torn into pieces, because of lack of family times together, or lack of paying attention to one's wife. Some men of God who are married to their ministries, and their ministerial partners lost all sensitivity to the emotional needs of their

Wives. They might even criticize her for complaining rather than showing some understanding to their ministerial commitments. After struggling for some time, such women try to leave the marriage. Without spending adequate time to listen to-, and reaching out to one's wife, she continues to drain off while her self-confidence and self-esteem is usually eroded, unless she continues to build them up in the LORD her strength, through His word and prayer. Yet, much of her self-security and confidence are built by her husband. I always understand a woman's marital position in her home when I observe her. A woman who has a sure place in her husband's life has so much inner confidence and resting posture even when you see her sitting down. The one that does not have a place in her husband's life is like someone looking for her identity, always staring at-, and at times admiring other women's relationship with their husbands in her heart. Some of such women lack self-confidence, no matter how famous they might be, while some of them become over-achievers to prove that they can do without their husbands. The word of God called a woman a weaker vessel, and asked men to give honor unto her: *Likewise, ye husbands, dwell with them according to knowledge, giving honour unto the wife, as unto the weaker vessel, and as being heirs together of the grace of life; **that your prayers be not hindered*** (1 Peter3:7). When a man toys with his wife's emotions and wellbeing, he is toying with his relationship with God. He risks praying and bringing offerings to God in vain. God will not hear him.

On a more personal note, every man needs to understand that there is different between a woman and a man. The way a woman understands a man's love language is different from the way the woman does. If a man does not have time to listen to his wife, and yet keeps telling her that he loves her, she will not take him serious. She sees love in a more practical way, as he supports her, spends quality time with her and emotionally supports her. Again, I recommend Dr Morris Chapman's book: *Five Love Languages* to every married couple, to understand how to express your love to your spouse the way he/she understands it. I personally added such note in my book: *How Do we invest in our children?* to also help parents understand how to express love to the children, the way they understand it. Let's continue to our line of thought.

A HUSBAND PROTECTS HIS WIFE'S WEAKNESS

A husband does not uncover his wife's weakness to her, to his people or to the world. He covers her with his strength. God equipped a man with so much strength, wisdom and grace to protect his wife and children from mistakes that will expose her weaknesses, or simply, he covers her weaknesses. We the Church were weak, naked, wretched and slaves of Satan. We were condemned to Hell. The LORD Jesus went to the Cross, died and shed His Blood for us, and purchased us to God. With the price (of His life), which He paid for our sins He covered our weaknesses, our nakedness with His righteousness, and sent His angels to guard and protect us from evil at all times (Psalm 34: 7; 91: 11). Revelation 19:7-8 says: Let us be glad and rejoice and give Him glory, for the marriage of the Lamb has come, and His wife has made herself ready." And to her it was granted to be arrayed in fine linen, clean and bright, for the fine linen is the righteous acts of the saints. The white linen is the very righteousness of Jesus Christ, which He gave us as a garment. He is our righteousness. We are justified by His own righteousness, not ours. Ours is like filthy rags before

God; He covers us with His own righteousness, which gives us right standing before God. We are therefore justified by His Blood.

Jesus Christ covers our weaknesses to the point that when we expose ourselves to danger, to shame and even make a mess of our lives and of ourselves, He brings us together, wipes away our shame and puts us back unto our feet, amen! Praise Him. Halleluiah! In the same way, a man covers his wife's shame and reproaches. I pointed earlier that the world, in most cases, sees a woman through her husband's eyes. If she is a piece of trash to her husband, that's how people see and treat her unless she has to stand up and fight for herself. But in fighting for herself, in most cases might even lose her reputation or be misunderstood. If, on the other hand, her husband honors and respects her regardless of how low or unequal to him he thinks she is, then people will esteem-, and respect her, just because her husband values her.

A FRIEND AND A CONFIDANT

This is closely related to the above. The Holy Spirit gave it to me after I had written everything, so I have to add this. When the LORD called me for a full time ministry, I asked Him how I was going to take care of my family seeing that my husband left us. He said to me that we are friends. Then, He explained to me that friendship is built on trust. If I cannot trust Him to take care of me and my children, how would He trust me with His anointing? Abraham trusted God that He would do what He said He would do, and God trusted Abraham that he would command his offspring in His way. God and Abraham were therefore, friends, and they built that friendship on trust Enoch and God were friends. This is what the Holy Spirit explained to me when he called me and said that as friends, let us trust each other.

In this same way, a husband is his wife's confidant and friend. A confidant is someone to whom one can always confide. Dictionary defines a confidant as a close friend, or associate to whom secrets are confided, or with whom private matters and problems are discussed. We mentioned earlier on the need to listen to one's wife, to pay attention to her, and to emotionally support her. When she has built this confidence that her husband always listens to her and builds and supports her, she will always confide in him knowing that he will never betray her confidence in him or trample on her concerns. Men are not to break their promises or their words to their wives. It hurts when a woman cannot trust her husband's very words. It could mean that his heart is not with her, or that he does not care how she feels when he breaks his words or promises, especially when it is something he always does. It is a bridge of trust. In Matthew 5: 37, the LORD Jesus says: But let your 'Yes,' be 'Yes', and your 'No,' be 'No", for whatever is more than these is from the evil one. As the head of the family, a man needs to understand that integrity is a good quality of a leader, and his children will understand that he is a man of integrity, and emulate him. God also honors the man that keeps his words.

Besides, there are instances when a woman would try to convince her husband of something very serious, or tries to reach out to him in her broken moments looking for emotional support, but he jokes it away, or pushes her away, or even criticizes her. For those men of God who are married to their ministries and their ministerial partners, such a man might criticize the wife of being insensitive or carnal or even, weak. By these, he continues to kill her confidence. Since she does not get the needed support from him, she might stop confiding in him, to avoid being criticized. All she needs is support, not to be criticized or have her

her weaknesses exposed to her. Here the man is not covering her, or building her up. As she nurses her wounds, she might start looking for a close friend with whom to confide. She is getting exposed to an outsider, which might ruin her.

Many mistakes some men also make, is relating something negative about their wives to their people. Remember, as I mentioned earlier in this book, a Pastor with a PHD, and many years in the ministry said to me that a wise woman will befriend her husband's people, and try to get them to love her, so that her husband can love her. In such a situation, the man begins to listen to his people, who probably did not like her. As he continues to communicate with his people, betraying his wife's confidence in him, if all he gets is negative reports from his people, he will eventually start maltreating her, which might lead to abuses and divorce. I have witnessed at least, three or four marriages that failed because of this betrayal of confidence.

A man visited Nigeria from the US, wedded his wife, and left her with his people while they work towards acquiring visa to join him later. Within six months of that wedding, it was over. His people were feeding him with negative reports about his new wife, which included that she scratched him off the picture she took with him. In another occasion, a man who had been living with his wife in the US for six years, and who had made money for him through her nursing profession (he too was making money), decided to visit home with his wife. While relating this to me, the wife said that he even bought her a flower, thanking her for all the money she made. This was before they left for Nigeria. He was probably communicating with his people before this time concerning his wife, while she was still living with him, betraying her. While in Nigeria together, they had a little misunderstanding, the man seized her documents and left her in the village and returned to the US. She was stranded. The next thing she saw was her mother in-law had left to be with her son in the US. She was still in Nigeria, trying to find her way back as her documents had been confiscated. His people convinced him to marry someone else because, she was not able to give him a baby within the six years they were married. Many women have been betrayed this way, and suddenly the marriage they hold so dear, crashed. The husband was in communication with someone outside the marriage. No matter what happens, you are to be your wife's best friend in whom she can always confide without fear of betrayal or criticism. Don't betray her confidence in you, and don't listen to outside opinion concerning her. Love is a voluntary thing, not emotion. You vowed at the altar to love her: for better for worse, for richer, for poorer, until death do you part.

> *Finally, be ye all of one mind, having compassion one of another, love as brethren, be pitiful, be courteous (1 Peter 3: 8).*

> *And be ye kind one to another, tenderhearted, forgiving one another, even as in Christ, God forgave you (Ephesians 4: 32.*

> *Be of the same mind one toward another. Mind not high things, but condescend to men of low estate. Be not wise in your own conceit (Romans 12: 16).*

Even if it is taking your wife some years to have a baby for you, don't let your people or outside pressure to destroy your home. Baby will come in God's timing. It is God that blesses with children. Abraham waited for twenty-five years before he received the Promised Seed; today he is the father of many nations. Rebecca waited for twenty years before she conceived for Esau and Jacob who became the father of Israel; Zachariah and Elizabeth were old before the LORD visited them with the birth of John the Baptist.

As long as you faithfully abide in Christ, and pray, it will happen one day. The LORD promised us that there shall none cast her young or be barren. All the barren women in the Bible including Hannah had babies. The only woman that remained barren was Michal, who disdained her husband David in her heart for dancing extravagantly before the LORD. The LORD blocked her womb for that. So then, don't let the need for child in your own expected timing to ruin your family. Some children come only after much prayer has been invested for their conception. Such situations occur because, God ordained to bring a Prophet or a unique vessel for His purpose through such couple. The names I mentioned above and Hannah, the mother of Samuel are such examples. Stay in prayers and thanksgiving for what the LORD planned to do among the nations, through your family. It is well! Let's quickly move to the next quality of a husband.

A PROVIDER

I once asked an American lady across my street, how she enjoys such a loving and wonderful home with her husband and three boys. She faithfully takes care of her boys, never hassles herself about money, but once in a while baby-sits a couple or more of neighbors' children. She has everything she needs including a nice car. She answered me that she and her husband agreed that the man provides for the family, and the woman keeps the home. So her husband provides for the family with all his heart and might, while the wife faithfully raises their children and does whatever our Father allows her to do. Her priority is caring for her family, building her home. She is a born-again Christian and so spends quality time teaching her boys the word of God. She makes money according to her capacity, but had all her needs met in her family through her husband's income.

In some cases, a woman can have a profession that yields her monthly income to support the family, but she has to do everything in such a way that her family comes first and is properly maintained; that her home is peaceful and welcoming. She makes sure the children always complete their homework, takes them to the library when there is need for that, and have adequate communication with their teachers for their academic, social and behavioral needs.

We discussed early that the love of money is the root of all evil. Many Nigerian women have been killed by their husbands here in the US, and when they are killed someone always asks: was she a Registered Nurse? There is a notion that such women act-up because they are the family breadwinners. These women became the breadwinners because the husbands wanted it so and, because the role has been switched. She became the man and could no longer act as a woman. This is not, however the case with many women who also provide for their families. If the LORD gives a woman the ability to provide for her family and support her husband and her family, it is a great blessing. We will address this area in her attitude in her divine role-play.

A man is not to ultimately depend on his wife for sustenance. God has given him the ability, strength and wisdom to provide for his family. I know a man, a Pastor who depends upon his wife for his needs, and outside the home, he tries to take advantage of women he meets, financially. His wife has a car; he doesn't drive it. As she continues to work even till night, he would be looking for someone to give him ride here and there. He lost the character, the authority the LORD gave him as a husband,

and begins to behave as a son to women he meets.

God equipped a man with much strength and wisdom and blesses the works of his hands, because of his family. He prospers any man that truly stands to provide for his family and continues to promote such a man. A man is never to be his wife's son. Women eventually get tired of mothering their husbands. Such a man eventually leaves the woman after losing his respect for her. The woman eventually feels used and dumped, while the man who used her does not have respect for her because she was there for that purpose, to be used.

The husband-son thing starts when the man marries a woman, because of her financial status, or what she has which the man needs. In some cases, such a woman might have lost her first marriage, has children; he steps in because he believes she needs a man. Most times, such men are younger than the women, or that may not be the case. They try to exploit their motherly compassion and use them as their means of getting to their aspired end. So in marriage, they will sit down there while their wives would hustle for the family. When a man takes this position in a marriage, he will not have the authority and the spiritual strength and wisdom the LORD gave to a man to take care of the family. A man is to be the head and the provider, and not let the wife work herself to exhaustion in order to provide for the family.

A woman that works herself to exhaustion (always working many shifts such as in nursing profession) sometimes loses her position as a homemaker and wife as we mentioned earlier. In some cases, she becomes hot-headed and stubborn. This leads to violence from the husband and marital instability. If the man however, can stand and take up the responsibility the LORD gave him to provide for his family, he will see the blessings of our Heavenly Father, who promises to command His blessings on whatever our hands touch. Such a man shall be respected in the society. Remember, God is the ultimate provider for the family, and He supplies all the needs of the family through any means He chooses specially when there is His order in the home.

From what the LORD was teaching me at that early morning concerning the roles of a man in the marriage, I understood that it is never the will of God for any of His daughter's to suffer in marriage, financially. Ruth the widow was married into the wealthy life of Boaz. That is how God planned the redemption of His daughters through marriage. Esther too, was married to the king of Persia. Most of the blessings that God pours in the marriage are for the wellbeing of the woman (whom He asks to be mostly keeper at home, and do whatever He allows her to do) and for the children. He makes most of such provisions through the man, the husband whom He guards with much strength and wisdom. He also promotes the man for his faithfulness. The man on the other hand would have the joy to see his family prospering with the provisions that come through him. Hard working for the family fulfills a man.

A FATHER

A woman's love is very nurturing, but a father's love is stricter and disciplinary in nature. The presence of a father in a home gives the woman the ability and the confidence to run her home with creativity and ease. The father instructs his children in the ways of the LOR; takes more firm stand in disciplining the children than the wife. His position as the father and the head of the home protects his wife from being attacked or disrespected by the children. I have met some families where a man would never tolerate his children's disobedience or disrespect to their wives. They don't sit down and watch the wife struggle with any of the children, but their intervention and disciplinary measures on such a child puts him/her under check. By that, he protects not just his wife from being abused by the children, but gives the children sense of direction on their attitudes. The best rod of correction for fathers to use mostly is the word of God. By this, the father is an instructor, a disciplinarian, and a protector for his family.

Both fathers and mothers are to protect the children from internal strife. They avoid this (internal strife) by avoiding the issue of favoring one person above others. When the parents begin to favor one child above the others, it creates jealousy, strife, competition and even hatred among the children. The children are very sensitive to this, and they can easily hurt the favored one. What happened to Joseph by his brothers because of their father's favoritism is not an old story. It continues to repeat itself. Even when the mother of the children begins to play favoritism to the one she loves most, the father, as the leader in the home, has to carefully demonstrate his love to every child equally. Many families are caught up with this game of favoritism, when they are not aware that they are even doing so. Let us be careful. It is serious, and the children can easily notice it.

My second child always accused me of favoring my firstborn most and treating her as my friend rather than one of them. That could be true due to how long both of us have come since her birth in Nigeria where we suffered many things together and came together here before the rest came. Probably, I was seeing her more understanding than others since she seemed to be acting very maturely and I trusted her with many responsibilities. Each time the second one complained anything against her, I never reacted well because I never saw her as would do anything to hurt any of her siblings. What I never knew was that they were fighting behind my back and the second one felt I was favoring the first above them. At times, I would yell at her in the middle of family prayers for a distractive attitude, but not knowing that her sister pinched her. She was looking like a trouble maker to me and people who came around us.

So she was inwardly bitter, yet I did not recognize that. As the first one entered University and we relocated to a different state, I wanted to transfer her to one of the Universities in our new location so she would be going from home and help me in my ministerial work, but the LORD said to me to retain her to her present school boarding house. He said that He wanted me to recognize something in my second born, which I have not recognized all these while. We have all considered her to be immature and babyish, and always babyish in behavior. Her complaints are never taken very serious. But as we moved from our new location to another location where the LORD transferred me for another new assignment, we began to go through some difficult experiences. She stood solidly as my backbone through prayers and strong faith. She has a strong prophetic spirit that sustained us through that period and very sensitive and sweet. I was beginning to truly discover her true personality. She is very caring, actually matured. But the bitterness she accumulated over the years of childhood "strife" with her sister which I never recognized and some other internal pains she stored in her heart over the years which included pains of school bullying, which I also never knew anything about, these began to surface. I had to struggle with her through these on her seventeenth year when she was entering University. She later understood that I love her and has been there for her. As a wonderful artist, she gave me my exact portrait as a surprised gift - wonderfully made. Right now, she is very caring, always caring for her siblings even from school and making sure I don't lose courage in any situation. She is a wonderful person and very strict with her faith in the

LORD. I always saw her sister more matured and responsible and trusted her with more things. She briefly felt left out in some things until I discovered her true personality and gifting. The day she presented to me a full artistic painting of my portrait on my birthday, I could not believe how she beautifully captured me like that, well detailed. That very day, I got into fight with her during prayers for persisting to lie down while the rest of us stood while praying. She left in the middle of the prayers, only to return to me after prayers with this beautiful portrait on which she'd been working for many hours…probably why she could not stand up during the prayers that night.

Every child is unique with different talents and graces. By God's grace, as we prayerfully pay attention to each of them we will discover that each of them is a unique blessing in our lives, and to the world as we help them develop according to God's plan for their lives.

Another way the father protects the family is to utilize his foresight. The word of God says that a prudent man foresees danger and hides himself (Proverbs 22:3). In spite of the burning hatred Jacob's love for Joseph created against him, yet he did not protect him from his brothers. He sent him with food to them, and to return to him with reports of what they did. Joseph did not know where his brothers were; he was wandering until a man saw him and directed him to Dothan, where they went. Eventually, Jacob did not see Joseph again until twenty years later. His brothers sold him into slavery, but convinced him that Joseph died. They brought to him his coat stained with animal blood. He hopelessly mourned for twenty long years for Joseph. He could have saved the situation by not letting Joseph wander about, looking for his brothers or sending him to the very brothers who hated him with passion. He could have seen some danger signs on that hatred.

A father is to weigh the decisions he makes for the family knowing that any decision he makes whether good or bad will impact his family. The word of God and prayers are always the safe place. My two books which I mentioned earlier are great tools for raising godly children.

A LEADER AND AN INSTRUCTOR

As a child, I remember my father always leading us to the altar of prayers before we sleep, each night instructing us with the word of God. He was a good Bible teacher. He used the word of God a lot in correcting and instructing us. When I had admission into a middle school very far from home, and was going to live in the school's boarding house, he called me that night and read out Psalm 91. He explained it to me line by line. He explained to me that though they would not be there to protect me, but anyone that dwells in the secret place of the Most High shall surely abide under His shadow, and His angels will keep and protect such a one. He prayed for me and committed me into the hands of God. That word stayed with me up till today. A father is to lead his family, to the LORD's altar and always teach them the word of God at all times, instructing them in the things of God. It was because of David's consistent instruction of the word to Solomon that caused Solomon to persistently advice the young people to heed the father's instruction.

Hear, ye children, the instruction of a father, and attend to know understanding (Proverbs 4: 1 KJV).

Hear my son, your father's instruction, and forsake not your mother's teaching (Proverbs 1: 8 ESV).

A wise son hears his father's
instruction... (Proverbs 13:1, ESV).

Mordecai's consistent instructions to Esther made her to become a wise woman, who knew how to make decisions for the contest. When she was asked to request for what she needed before going to the King, she rather asked for whatever Haggai, the King's Eunuch in charge of the King's concubines suggested. She thus won the favor of everyone that saw her. The King also favored her and made her the Queen, in place of Vashti (Esther 2:15-16).

In the King' palace, Esther continued to follow the godly instructions of Mordecai. Through her obedience to Mordecai and faith in God, she took the decision that led to the deliverance of the life of her cousin Mordecai, and also the entire people of God in the land of Persia, when Haman determined to wipe out all the Jews. She obeyed Mordecai the way she obeyed him when he was raising her up. The LORD God commands parents to consistently instruct the children: *You shall teach them diligently to your sons and shall talk of them when you sit in your house and when you walk by the way and when you lie down and when you rise up (Deuteronomy 6: 7, 11).* God said concerning Abraham: *For I have chosen him, that he may command his children and his household after him to keep the way of the LORD by doing righteousness and justice, so that the LORD may bring to Abraham what he has promised him (Genesis 18: 19).*

Your godly instructions to your children will stay with them through every situation of life and help them fulfill their destinies. The godly instructions of Jacob to his sons before Joseph was sold into slavery, kept him in the fear of God, through thirteen years of slavery and imprisonment until the LORD exalted him as the second in command in Egypt. He continued steadfastly therein until the LORD united him with his brothers. He said to them that it was not in his place to revenge for what they did to him. Vengeance belongs to the LORD. He however, assured them that God allowed the situation so that he would keep them alive during the seven years of the famine (emphases mine). The wisdom with which he handled every situation, was because of the instructions he received earlier from his father Jacob, as a youth. The word of God kept him through good and bad times.

As a leader in the family, the man is to see to it that the family is protected from crises and when problem arises with the wife, he brings the wife to order, always assuring her of his love for her as Christ consistently assures us of His love, and companionship. Even when we go astray and are discouraged, He still takes the lead to find us and bring us back to Himself. He said that of all the Father committed into His hands, no one shall snatch them out of His hands (John 10: 28). He is a good Shepherd, and is therefore able to keep us till the end. In this same way, the father and the husband needs to see to it that he keeps his family together through prayers and the word, and physically seeing to their total well-being. You are not in competition with your wife, but you are her leader, her head, her cover, and provider; also you are a father and a cover to your children. It is a huge responsibility, but God's grace is sufficient for you.

A man is never to use his role as the major authority of the home to abuse his wife and children, or to force submission on her even when he is wrong. He is to submit to Christ as Christ is submitted to God, and to love his wife as Christ loved the Church and gave Himself for her. Every decision he makes in the family has to be in line with the word of God, in agreement with his wife and for the good of the family. What causes crises at times in families is when the man begins to make decisions based on his egos, abusing the authority the LORD gave him. Your wife is your partner, your fellow joint-heir of the manifold grace of God. Without her, you will not fully succeed. Honor her, respect her, and value her input. Don't trash her, or put her off looking for opinion from outside. The opinions you will get from outside your marriage might not be the right counsel and so is bound to perish. Your wife is ordained, and anointed to be your help-meet. Allow her to play that role in your life. Teach her how to do it well. Work with her, pray consistently with her and you will fulfill God's plan for your family.

QUALITY TIME

I will like to add the need for quality times among couples. For years, the Holy Spirit continued to impress this subject over and over in my mind. He continues to tell me that the way to grow intimacy with God is to learn to spend good quality times with Him. When we spend many hours each day in His presence both in studying the word and in fellowshipping with Him through prayers and worship; we continue to partake of Him, growing deeper in knowing Him as Paul desired to know Him, and into His likeness. We are therefore, changed from glory to glory (2 Corinthians 3: 18). In the same way, God expects every man to learn to spend quality times with his wife each day, or each time. It is in spending quality times with each other that you grow intimately in understanding and in partaking of each other. You listen to -, and learn to flow with each other's heartbeat. Growing intimately with each other in Christ will bring both of you into such a union that you live and think as one, fulfilling the word of God that you are to be in one accord with each other. Since you are achieving this intimacy with each other in Christ, which is the ultimate plan of God to bring your unity into complete unity with Himself, with Christ and the Holy Spirit ((John 17: 21), the covering of

The glory of the LORD will cause you to enjoy the fullness of His protection, love and provision.

THE GODLY ROLE OF A WOMAN IN MARRIAGE

Wives, submit yourselves unto your own husbands, as unto the LORD. For the husband is the head of the wife, even as Christ is the head of the church: and he is the savior of the body. Therefore, as the church is subject unto Christ, so let the wives be to their own husbands in everything (Ephesians 5: 22-23)

Likewise, ye wives, be in subjection to your own husbands; that, if any obey not the word, they also may without the word be won by the conversation of the wives; While they behold your chaste conversation coupled with fear. Whose adorning let it not be that outward adorning of plaiting the hair, and of wearing of gold, or of putting on of apparel. But let it be the hidden man of the heart, in that which is not corruptible, even the ornament of a meek and quiet spirit, which is in the sight of God of great price. For after this manner in the old time the holy women also, who trusted in God, adorned themselves, being in subjection unto their own husbands; Even as Sara obeyed Abraham, calling him LORD: whose daughters ye are, as long as ye do well, and are not afraid with any amazement (1 Peter 3: 1-6)

SUBMISSION

God requires a woman to be submissive to her husband. He mentioned this in few places in the Bible. She has left her parents and cleaved to her husband. Her submission or subjection to him is part of a divine order in a home. God is the founder of the home, and it is only in following His order for the home that a marriage succeeds. In every organization or institution, there is always a head, who is accountable to the overall boss. That head in the family is the husband, and he is accountable to God for the success or the failure of the marriage. The woman therefore, is to prayerfully submit to his leadership in all things, because the man himself is subjected to Christ as his head, and the children will follow this lead.

The word of God emphasizes that the woman is to submit to her husband so that if any obey not the word, that's if your husband is an unbeliever, he will without the preaching of the word by mouth, see it in the character of the woman, and be won to God. Obedience to one's husband is obedience to God and it brings her under divine protection and provision. The husband, as the head of the home, exercises authority over the wife. Authority goes with responsibility. As the head of the woman, it is his responsibility to protect, provide and see to her overall wellbeing. But, for the woman to stay under divine coverage and provision, and not under God's anger, she has to stay under the authority of her husband, submitting to his leadership, respecting and honoring him. The husband and wife, joined together in Christ is a three-fold chord, which the word says, is not easily broken. The glory of God protects them as long as they stay under this unity and

submission. The husband being submitted to Him as his head honors Christ by walking in obedience to His word. The woman therefore, submitting to her husband,
is under divine coverage. That is also why the LORD asked the children to obey their parents because it is the right thing to do, so they will live long and be prosperous in life (Ephesians 1:1-2). Disobedience and rebelliousness by the wife or children, removes them from divine coverage and they are exposed to satanic attacks. That's why many children or young people die prematurely. Most of them believe they are "grown-ups", and have no need to obey
parents, anymore. And so the enemy lures them out of divine order and they become exposed to his manipulations and attacks. Whenever children or young people begin to rebel against parental authority, God expects the parents to stand in the gap for them so that through their prayers, God's mercy will protect and cover them until they return to their divine cover. Divine order is maintained in the home as the woman learns to submit to her husband.

I always want to touch many realistic situations of life so that someone will learn from it. The subject of submission has drawn out many controversies. At times, the man will argue that the LORD God asked the woman to submit first, before the man will love her. To this I remind them the word that says that Christ loved the Church and gave Himself for her, even when the church was not yet born. Isaiah asked: Who can declare His generation? (Isaiah 53: 8) Christ love brought him down from glory, from Heaven to Earth to the sinful world. He died for the people, who later scattered and denied him after three years of teaching and mentoring them. John said that we love Him, because He first loved us and gave His life for us. The word of God therefore, asked a man to love his wife as Christ loved the Church and gave Himself for her. The man's unconditional devotion and love for the woman draws out a response in a godly woman, to love and reverence him. She feels secured with him and trusts him to be there for her, as her close friend, brother and confidant. So the submission is as unto the LORD, and this is pleasing to the LORD.

The model of a wife's submission to her husband is as Christ subjected Himself unto the Father. She is not to abuse her husband's love and devotion to her, but with fear and reverence to her God, submits and help-meets him. This takes us to another question on when to submit and when not to submit. Is the wife to submit in everything, even when it contradicts the word of God?

I once asked a question in a Church sometime in 1990 on the issue of telling lies in the family. I quoted a scripture that referred us as Sarah's daughters. She obeyed Abraham and called him LORD. So, when Abraham asked her to say to the King of Egypt that she was his sister (not his wife), she did the same. Actually, she was also his sister, but the situation made room for the King of Egypt to take Sarah as wife. I believed however, that Abraham, the godly man and the leader of the home dealt with the situation in prayers, which caused God to intervene for her. The Pastor however, explained the issue of Ananias and Sephirah where both couples agreed to lie in the Church and were both slain by the Holy Spirit (Acts 5). The issue here is; submission has to be in the will of God. We submit first to the LORD. Whenever a husband requires a wife to do the wrong thing with him, and expects the wife to submit to him, the LORD by the Holy Spirit intervenes and asks the woman not to comply. The man has gone out of divine order, and wants to lead the wife to the wrong part he has chosen. In such a case, the Holy Spirit, who might have been dealing with the man without him submitting to the word of God, would not allow the woman to go through with the same rebellion. If Sephira had refused to agree with her husband in lying to the Holy Spirit, both of them would probably be alive as the husband would not have had the confidence to go through with his lies without his wife's support. In such a case, the woman is rather helping her husband submit to the counsel of the Holy Spirit because; the LORD Jesus is his LORD. We are all accountable to the LORD. We are all serving the LORD. The man is not a master, who demands total submission to his subjects/slaves, but it is in love that the Church submits to Christ. He shed His Precious Blood and took our place on the cross, and died for us. He took away our wretchedness and clothed us with His garment of righteousness and holiness. He is our very present help in trouble, our Maker our Husband. We love Him and submit to him purely out of deep love and appreciation, not out of compulsion. Our submission to Him brings us into total unity and oneness with Him and the Father, and we share in His glory with the Father (John 17: 20-23), and nothing shall be impossible to us.

In the same way, a woman is to submit to her husband, with meekness and gentleness of spirit and not to be bullied into it. If she is being bullied into it, she might become manipulative and rebellious. But love answers it all, praise God. That is why the LORD commands the man to love her as Christ loved the Church and gave himself for her; to love her (the wife) as he loves himself, nourishing and cherishing her.

A GENTLE AND A MEEK SPIRIT

This is the spirit that characterizes a godly woman. As she submits to her husband, praying fervently for him and her children in her private times, she continues to partake of the image of Jesus since the submission is unto the LORD.

When the word says, let not your beauty be that of putting on of apparel, with braided her, and jewelries ... It does not mean that the LORD condemns any of that. The LORD is saying that you are not to give priority to the outward beauty, but to the inward beauty that is formed through the putting on of the LORD Jesus Christ, and letting Him clothe you with the precious and glorious character of the Holy Spirit. The characters of the Holy Spirit are love, joy peace, patience kindness, goodness, gentleness, faithfulness and self-control (Galatians 5: 22). These are the fruits that are more precious to God than silver and gold, or any outward beauty. Concerning the outward beauty, it is written that charm is deceitful, beauty is vain, but a woman that fears the LORD, she shall be praised. In Psalm 45: 13, King's daughter is all glorious within: her clothing is of wrought gold. In verse 2, he says: *thou art fairer than the children of men: grace is poured into thy lips. Therefore, God has blessed thee forever... all thy garments smell of myrrh, and aloes, and cassia out of the ivory palaces whereby they made thee glad.*

When we talk of myrrh, which is a sweet smelling spice before the LORD, myrrh bespeaks of self-sacrifice as we noted earlier when we looked into Esther's preparation with the bitter but the sweet-smelling oil of myrrh. That is when the LORD Jesus says: forget also your own people, your father's house, so that the king will delight in you. This verse also applies to the marriage union between a husband and a wife. The woman will have to forget her people and their influence in her life. This becomes part of her sacrificial journey in the marriage. It does not say that she does not have anything to do with her people anymore in life, but it means they don't influence her anymore. Her life and decisions are with her husband. She is in one accord with him.

As she presses on to please her ultimate Husband and Master the LORD Jesus Christ in her marriage, in obedience and submission to her husband even in the most difficult circumstances, always seeking the face of the LORD, she continues to be clothed and beautified with Christ. Through patience and long suffering, the characters of the Holy Spirit will begin to radiate through her. Her meekness, gentleness and quietness but with knowledge and wisdom is being noticed by her companion, her husband and even by people outside her home. She is adorning herself with the characters of Christ, which causes her robe (her righteousness), her characters to smell like precious spices before God. The LORD Jesus Christ, her ultimate Bridegroom, delights greatly in her because, by the fruits of her walk with God, she is bringing pleasure to our Heavenly Father. This is why the word of God said: let not your adorning be physical, but spiritual adorning, which makes you attractive to Christ, covering you with His glory and honor and ultimately you will win your unbelieving husband, if he desires.

As a young person, our choir mistress at a point in her life considered her age as getting old, and desired at all costs to get married. She therefore, suddenly left the Church contrary to the rules of the Assemblies of God Church, which enforces marriage only within the ministry. She married a Catholic man. That was a complete fall away. The situation created too much problems to some members of our Church, who tried to advise her to do, otherwise. The ministry, at the time, was very strict to the point that we were not allowed to use make ups or paint our nails, but suddenly she started doing all these things. Her heart was not however, at peace even in that marriage. The man loved her very much, but he would not let her attend Assemblies of God Church, anymore.

She was blessed with many sons in that marriage, up

to five or more. That was a pride for an African man. After about six years of her continual quiet agony before the LORD, the man released her to worship the LORD with her Church, where they lived at the time. Two years later, in her faithful obedience and submission to the man, he released the children to join her in worshiping the LORD with the Assemblies of God ministry. As time went on, all of them were won over to the LORD. So when I was sent to Enugu state to live with the in-laws, I met her in the Church with her husband and children. She later explained her story to me. By her submission, meekness, patience, obedience and gentleness coupled with consistent prayers and (probably) fasting too, she won her husband and children to the LORD, even without the preaching of the word by mouth to them.

I also met another couple as a student in the University of Calabar, Nigeria. I had a roommate whose brother's wife also worshipped with a good Pentecostal Church. She was a Pharmacist, but her husband, a Veterinary Doctor, did not have anything to do with that. The sister, my roommate said to me that the situation of the wife not dressing in a worldly manner as the husband wanted was not funny to the husband. We visited the family; she was gentle, meek, hardworking and very prayerful. She was faithful. One night in her prayers, the LORD revealed to her that robbers were in her husband's clinic. She called her husband up and with some police officers they went there, the robbers already left. They gathered all their stuff, but left everything behind. They left with nothing. Eventually, through her virtuous and precious character, her husband was won over to the LORD.

God warned His people not to be unequally yoked with unbelievers; never to marry them. Many women however, met the LORD after the marriage. They need to win their family over to the LORD. When they put on such characters of Christ, allowing the life of Christ to be manifested through them as we described above, the LORD will honor their faith and touch their husbands' hearts. That's why the word of God says that they could win their husbands through their attitudes, not by merely preaching the word to them.

The reason many husbands are not won by the beautiful characters of their wives is that, they have a different mindset in the marriage and simply don't want to see the woman excel in life. It could be the issue of competition, worldliness or abuse. He could also be an agent of Satan assigned to destroy the woman. This is a situation which one Pastor often says that a marriage where the man and the woman are headed to opposite directions, no matter how fast the man runs to the East and the woman to the West, there is no meeting point for the two. If the husband's assignment is to destroy the woman, there is nothing she will do to make things right. Her virtuous characters, will not win the man over because he is under a different influence and assignment.

When a man, who supposed to love and protect his family, begins to destroy them, and refuses to repent or change; as the woman remains faithful and committed in honoring him, fearing the LORD and interceding for the family, God knows how to sovereignly fix the situation. He has a purpose in everything. We trust His wisdom and sovereignty in everything. He asked Hosea to marry Gomer, a harlot to show His people the kind of relationship they had with Him. In this case, Hosea's marital experience was used as a symbol of what the people of Israel were doing to God, their Husband. Their harloting under trees and stones, worshipping foreign gods was compared to Gomer's prostitution as she was always running after her lovers. The LORD sometimes allows certain marriages to pass through many challenges for a purpose of some things He wants to teach His people.

My marital experiences equipped me with the rich knowledge I have now on the perils of tradition which entered into the house of God, affecting Gods plan and purposes for families, and the pains and uncertainties of living with a man that never loves his wife, but lives deceitfully with her. I would not have been able to address the issues I am addressing in this book; I would not have been able to understand the dilemmas of most women, especially African women in marriage even in the Church. As I travel to other countries in ministry, I minister with complete understanding of what they might be experiencing. Also the experiences and such exposures helped me to understand that there is so much witchcraft in the House of God. To serve God in spirit and in truth, you will be severely persecuted by false brethren. The Church is full of tares and wheat growing together, but the LORD has a harvest time for them. So even in marriage, one has to let the LORD direct him or her in order not to fall into the hands of wrong person (check out the companion of this book (upcoming): *Before You Get Married*).

At a time in marriage however, the LORD might remove such a man from the woman's life so she can raise the godly children He sought out of their union in the fear of God and continue to fulfill her divine destiny in Christ.

KEEPERS AT HOME

One of the roles the LORD assigned to women is to love their husbands and be keepers at home. It is written that a good woman builds her home, but the foolish tears it down with her hands. The beauty and the comfort of a home is a good woman. The comfort or the discomfort of her home depends on how she builds her home.

Many women abandon the building of their homes to their house-keepers, and risk losing their husbands to them. This happens mostly in some third world countries where it is cheap to employ house-helps, even for free of charge. Most of these people become expert at home-making because they were given such roles of building the home by their house mistresses.

In proverbs 31, the Bible addresses the role of a virtuous woman in home-making/home-building. I was invited to minister somewhere a couple of years ago on *The Productive Woman*, I looked into the areas a woman can build a good home and still be productive in other areas of life. We looked into the issue of discovering her talents and moving into such direction since the word of God says that a man's gift makes room for him and brings him before great men. Many women take up professions that place so much demand on their times to the extent that they cannot take care of their families. In some cases, most of such women are the breadwinners of their homes, while their husbands don't do much, or he tries to take up the role of keeping the home since the wife is the breadwinner. In other cases, they are both making good monies and their best alternative is hiring a homemaker for the family. This is not the will of God for families. A man is supposed to provide for his family, while the wife pays more attention to building the home, because the LORD equipped her with anointing and grace to build her home, nurture the children with her love and godly character, and make her home, a home for her household.

In Proverbs 31, we see that she does not work outside her home (I am not asking those who have job to quit their jobs and work from home, but if you see such opportunity it will be great). Her priority is first of all her God, then her family, before her profession. She works willingly with her hands – doing what she is talented to do, which does not interfere with her duty for her household. Her talent will make room for her, and the LORD promises to bless the works of her hands. It is a covenant promise. In Deuteronomy 28: 8 it is written that the LORD will command the blessing upon you in your barns and in all that you put your hand to, and he will bless you in the land which the LORD your God gives you. When a woman sets her priority right before God, she will experience the blessings of God in her life and family. At times, the LORD promotes her husband in the area of his job so that he continues to adequately provide for his family. A woman is to work willingly with her hands depending on the talent with which she is endowed. One way to discover one's God-given talent is to find out what you do that gives you such a great fulfillment. I enjoy writing. It gives me great joy as the Holy

Spirit continues to inspire me and releases words full of wisdom as I write. At times when I read what I write, I realized I did not write it, but the LORD used my hands to do it. My first book took me to many places I would not ordinarily go, and some preaching appointments which I never even planned. Then it became a book of the month for one of the inspiration radio stations whereby I had live interviews and Bible study hours on those radio stations. I simply wrote the book the LORD gave me to write, and it started opening doors for me. Then I started digressing into businesses. It worked a while, but messed up the path the LORD was opening for me until I returned to Him with repentance, after several warnings. I am still moving according to the pattern He mapped out for me, now.

God is serious concerning the gifts and the talents with which He endowed every one, and He expects us to run with them, and bear fruits with them. Then you will experience fulfillment both in your personal life and that of your family, for the gift of God will enable you to fulfill your call both as a mother and as a woman of God. The Proverbs 31 woman seeks wool and flax and works willingly with her hands, depending on her response to her gifting from the LORD. The LORD blessing the works of her hands, she lives above others, bringing her food from afar and making investments. She is productive. Her productivity does not have to take her away from her household; she did not have to give her children to a babysitter to care for her for twelve hours a day in order for her to make money. She girds her loins with strength and strengthens her arms; she lays her hands to the spindle, and her hand holds the distaff (Vs. 17, 19). She is very hard-working, and while at that, she uses the money she makes from her hard work to invest in the family and helps to provide for her household. In verse 27, it is written that she looks well to the wellbeing of her household, and eats not the bread of idleness. We talked about her hardworking spirit, which yields her much profit for the well-being of her family. She buys for her household, rich and appropriate clothing to suit each season of the year, and also takes very good care of herself with "purple and silk clothing", which shows that she does not eat bread of idleness, or getting things "As – is", or just from thrift stores. She works hard; God blesses her works and so she gets her supplies from afar...from good places.

The virtuous woman rises up early and gives meat to her household and a portion to her maidens. This says that her house-maid does not run her family for her. She prepares what everyone (including her maidens) eats. This gives her room to carefully prepare healthy foods for the family at all times. When she has seen to the well-being of her family, she takes off for her duty for the day. It could be her ministerial work; it could be for some business with which she is involved, but her house-help only takes care of what she appoints her to do. She does not do it all.

I will like to mention some more essential things she does. The word says that her candle does not go out at night. She spends time at night fellowshipping with the LORD, and making prayers and supplications according to the will of God. She is a watchman (an intercessor) both for her family and for others, which the LORD brings to her attention. She is a co-laborer with the LORD, while still raising her children and help-meeting her husband. It could also mean that, because of her constant devotion to the LORD, she has extra oil in her lamp like the five wise virgins to keep her household together even in times of difficulties. She is full of the Holy Spirit, and watches out against the wolves afar off, before they approach to attack her family. Her lamp being full of oil and in her constant watchfulness through prayers, she can discern divine timing, and be able to prepare for abundance like Joseph so that they can survive both in times of prosperity and in times of draught.

Her model lifestyle brings great respect for her husband outside the home, because people watch her lifestyle, the fruit of her works even in the lives of her children. She fully respects her husband and he has no need to stay away from home, each day, but always comes home to be with her. She is his lover, friend and confidant. She opens her mouth with knowledge, and so the fruit of her lips feeds many including her husband. Her home is like heaven to her household, because of her beauty of character, knowledge and virtuous lifestyle. She is also a mother to the community as many people try to imitate her lifestyle, and feed from the fruit of her lips, from the wisdom and the knowledge that come through her.

FEARING GOD

The woman we described above is a woman that fears and reverences God. Such reverence kept her within the will of God, and the LORD is her strength and wisdom. Her children follow in her footsteps and honor their father and mother which is well pleasing to the LORD, and which is the secret of their long life and prosperity (Ephesians 6: 1-3). The word of God says that she shall be praised, because of the qualities we described above. Her praise is not because of what she achieved financially, but because of the fear and the reverence of the LORD which is the guiding principles of her life.

So many women are problems in other people's families because of what they contribute to their own families. They could be holding professional jobs, running successful businesses, paying their mortgages, working many shifts to provide financially for the family while other women who don't achieve as they do are seen as lazy, and under-achievers. Some of such women at times, create problems for some women who have not done as much as they do.

We have discussed at length what it takes to become a virtuous woman, and what makes for beauty and excellence in the presence of God: a meek and a quiet spirit. You don't have to bother yourself with what you don't have. Don't compare yourself with other women, and don't allow yourself to be intimidated by what other people are doing or what they have. Most of the people who are considered successful are not happy and contented people. We discussed that earlier. Paul says that godliness with contentment is great gain (1Timothy 6: 6). In spite of what most of such people have, they don't experience fulfillment of life, because the life of a man does not consist on the abundance of things which he possesses (Luke 12: 15). Don't worry if the other woman is paying her mortgage, sponsoring all her children in the best schools and the husband is boasting about it. It does not matter if she is the one marrying her husband, rather than her husband marrying her. You don't even know how she got to where she is. It also does not matter if such a family is walking in the fear of the LORD, and such blessings upon her life are a great joy. That is her season. However, the word of God did not say that it is the woman that does all that, that shall be praised, but it is the woman that fears the LORD that shall be praised (Proverbs 31: 30). It is the woman that fears the LORD and also teaches her children the fear of the LORD that shall be praised. The fear of God is a fountain of life. It is the beginning of wisdom. Wisdom is profitable to direct. It will teach you how to build your home, how to profit and also how to help - meet your husband. The Holy Spirit makes a woman virtuous. It is not an overnight experience. It is a progressive work of the Holy Spirit in the life of the one, who is cooperating with Him. So in partnering with Him and in His counseling and might, you will excel according to God's planning and timing for your life and family, not according to expectations of the society or others. Always set your priorities right and partner with the Holy Spirit. The model of the woman we discussed is the woman God expects to raise among His daughters.

Chapter 8

PRAYERS

We cannot over-emphasize the need for prayer for a successful marriage. First of all, the search for the marriage partner started with prayers. The word of God says that houses and riches are inheritance of parents, but a prudent woman is from the LORD. Again, it is written: who can find a virtuous woman? for her price is far above rubies (Proverbs 31:10). It means that for someone to have married the right person, to have found the prudent woman that God desired for him, he might have knocked on the heart of God. Such a woman lives in the Heart of God, and that's where such a man knocked until the LORD released her to him. We talked more on this on Before You Get Married. This means that the marriage started by faith. It started by receiving from the hands of the LORD the man or the woman He ordained for you.

The marriage is founded in Christ, and it will take prayers and the word of God to build it. While bad words, curses, negative criticisms and strife are like pouring venoms or acid at the foundation of marriage, which in turn pollutes and erodes the foundation, prayers and the word of God cultivates and causes it to grow.

I will quickly like us to check one of the most effective ways we can address our prayers in our marriage. I know that in Divine role Play, we mentioned that the candle of a virtuous woman does not go out at night. The night means trying times, drought or simply midnight hours of prayers. In whatever way we see the night, she learns to travail until she receives her answers. Because she is alone with God, her maker, her Husband, the source of her wisdom and strength, she always knows what next step God wants her to take. Also, God reveals a lot to her concerning each member of her family. She always prevails through prayers.

Prayers have to be targeted and made to hit the bull's eye. The word of God says that we do not receive answers, because we prayed amiss. Someone taught me how to pray with the word when I was languishing in frustration awaiting visa while years were rolling by; I wanted to give up on the marriage since we had not yet wedded. As soon as I started praying the word just as the lady advised me, instantly I started seeing results, and my wedding took place. That was in 1991. From then on, the weapon of the Word of God became one of my effective weapons of warfare. So then, one of the most effective ways to pray and continue to pray for our families is praying the word of God. The word does not fail. God says to Jeremiah that He watches over his words to perform it (Jeremiah 1:12). The word of God proceeds from Him, comes down to Earth and then returns to Him. But He says that His word will not return to Him void; it must accomplish the purpose for which it is sent. This is what He meant when He said to Jeremiah that He watches over his word to perform it.

The angels of God constantly perform those word you consistently pray or speak concerning your marriage and concerning every member of your family. My book: *Raising Godly Children: Foundation Laid In Prayers* is a great handbook on praying and speaking the word of God over the lives of the children, and every member of the family. When you begin to consistently speak and apply the word of God in your prayers and in your daily lives concerning your marriage and every member of the family, the word will surely work for you. The secret of success which the LORD God gave to Joshua was that the book of the law shall not depart out of his mouth, but he was to meditate on it day and night, so that he would be careful to do according to all that is written therein, for then he would make his way prosperous and have good success (Joshua 1:8). David in Psalm 1 emphasized that the man, who meditates on the word of God day and night shall surely be blessed, and flourish like the tree planted by the rivers of water, whose leaves never withers. The people of God, like such trees bear their fruits in their seasons and whatsoever they do, they prosper. The Angels of God, who perform the word of God, which God's people speak, will always work on the words of your prayers which you pray as you daily pray and meditate on the word of God. This will cause both you and every member of your family to prosper. Remember that your family is a family of God, and He makes His investments in the lives of every member therein.

Another effective way to pray is praying in tongues. This allows the Holy Spirit to intercede for us, and with us concerning deep things of our lives and families which we could not discern with our understanding. It is written that the spirit also helps our weakness; for we do not know how to pray as we should, but the Spirit Himself intercedes for us with groaning too deep for words; and he who searches the hearts knows what the mind of the Spirit is, because He intercedes for the saints according to the will of God (Romans 8: 26-27).

We talked earlier that a father is the leader to lead the family to the altar of prayers. He is the Priest of his household, and thus performs his priestly duties when he does that. There is a proverb that says that the family that prays together stays together. The LORD referred me to Isaiah 56;1-7, as the model of the family of the people of of God. I later understood that this is the set-up of Jewish families. The husband and the father of the home, as the Priest is required to establish a family altar where the entire family gathers each day for prayers and thanksgiving unto God. Let's see how Isaiah 56 applies to our families;

Thus says the LORD: "Keep justice, and do righteousness, For My salvation is about to come, And My righteousness to be revealed. Blessed is the man who does this, And the son of man who lays hold on it; Who keeps from defiling the Sabbath, And keeps his hand from doing any evil." Do not let the son of the foreigner, Who has joined himself to the LORD Speak, saying, "The LORD has utterly separated me from His people"; Nor let the eunuch say, "Here I am, a dry tree." For thus says the LORD: "To the eunuchs who keep My Sabbaths, And choose what pleases Me, And hold fast My covenant, Even to them I will give in My house And within My walls a place and a name Better than that of sons and daughters; I will give them an everlasting name That shall not be cut off. "Also the sons of the foreigner Who join themselves to the LORD, to serve Him, And to love the name of the LORD, to be His servants— Everyone who keeps from defiling the Sabbath, And holds fast My covenant— Even them I will bring to My holy mountain, And make them joyful in My house of prayer. Their burnt offerings and their sacrifices Will be accepted on My altar; For My house shall be called a house of prayer for all nations." The LORD God, who gathers the outcasts of Israel, says, "Yet I will gather to him Others besides those who are gathered to him (Isaiah 56: 1-7).

Our family is a gift from the LORD, and the LORD Jesus is the head of our homes. Our houses are His house, and so, it is His mount Zion, the city of God. *But you have come to Mount Zion and to the city of the living God, the heavenly Jerusalem, to an innumerable company of angels,* (Hebrews 12: 22). The glory of God is the covering of our homes. Isaiah 4:5, *And the LORD will create upon every dwelling place of mount Zion, and upon her assemblies a cloud and a smoke by day, and the shining of a flaming fire by night; for upon all the glory shall be a defense.* English Standard version called that last word: a canopy while some other Bible versions call it, a covering. Our homes have the covering of the glory of God upon it, a defense for every member of the family.

As the Holy Mountain of God, His angels encompass our houses, and like Jacob's ladder, they ascend and descend in our homes, because we have an altar of prayers within. Every evening and every morning, we ought to come to the presence of God with every member of our families unto the altar of the LORD to give Him praise and thanksgiving offering, for He is the LORD of creation who created both evening and morning. We worship Him for we are made for that purpose to bring Him glory and honor (Revelation 4: 10). As the day also breaks each day, He expects the head of the family to bring the family unto the altar of prayers for the sacrifice of thanksgiving and praise. One day around 4:00am, the LORD opened my ears and I heard every creation both great and small including ants, all bringing praises to God. Stars, moon and everything was worshipping God, and I heard the sounds of their praises. Everything that

God created brings Him glory and honor each breaking of the day. He asked me to join them. He is worthy of our praises each morning, as each morning unfolds with it His new mercies, new blessings, new beginning for each of His creation. As the flowers unfold their leaves, the trees clap their hands and the sun begin to rise with healing in its wings, we joyously join all creation to bring unto Him a thanksgiving offering, while we also order the day according to His will so that the dayspring will shake the wicked out of their place. God therefore, expects every family to come to the altar of praises and thanksgiving each morning to worship Him and to receive the blessings and direction for the day. The same thing happens each evening. The Bible says that evening and morning was the first day, the same the second day. By doing this each day, we are fully walking with Him in our marriages and families, and we shall experience His glory, His joy and the fullness of His blessings over our families, and over every member of our families.

We see that Jewish people always prosper and excel in whatever they do; it is because they keep the LORD's order and statutes as described above. They strictly observe the Sabbath which begins on Friday evening. They gather in their family sanctuaries on Friday evenings, and begin to worship and give thanks to God of creation, Who finished His work and rested on the Sabbath. They celebrate Him, worship Him and break bread and wine before Him and eat in the presence of the LORD. After this, they share their meal which is feasting with the LORD. All the conversation at this time is centered in thanksgiving for the goodness of the LORD, memory verses and words of praises are shared. After the meal, they continued to celebrate the LORD.

The LORD Jesus says that where two or three are gathered in His name, He is also there. The celebration therefore, causes the presence and the blessings of the LORD to be upon their families. This is the order of their lives. They observe the prayer ordinances the LORD gave them, His Feasts, the daily reading of the word of God on each family gathering. All these are led by the father of the house, who is the Priest of the family. The LORD God therefore, expects families to do the same with the father leading as the Priest of the family. These replace arguments, fighting and strife. As we continue to come to the altar of prayers each night and day, the word of God says that upon mount Zion shall be deliverance, and there shall be holiness; and the house of Jacob shall possess their possessions (Obadiah 1: 1. The altar of prayers in our families becomes a place to possess our possessions, the blessings of the LORD for us each day.

Also, from the above scriptures, it is written that our houses, the House of God shall be called The House of prayers for all nations. The word of God encourages us to practice hospitality. My earthly father had a very large house in our village. During Nigeria-Biafra war, many people who fled war in their state filled our village. He opened our house and made it a city of refuge for most of these people. Our house was filled with people. Our large, living room became their bedroom. Even after the war, my father continued to use our house as a shelter for many people, who needed temporary residence. In all these, he always brought these people unto the altar of prayers and the word of God. The foreigners, the people that never knew God, as he was opening doors for them, he would also bring them to the altar of prayers and the word of God. He was a deacon and a Sunday School teacher in our local Church. When the church needed to establish a branch in our village, our living room became the Church until they finally built a structure for the Church.

Our families are expected to be a place of salvation

and deliverance; a place where people will find solution to their problems at the altar of prayers. It is a place to raise our children and prepare them as the LORD's army for the next generation. They will walk in divine favor as the presence of God continues to go with them. The glory of the LORD continues to be a canopy over them.

There are times the family begins to face trying times and challenges. At times, the enemy tries to turn one of the spouses against the other. In some cases, it's teen rebelliousness or financial draught, let us not depart from the altar of sacrifice of praise, thanksgiving and prayers for therein we will find answers, hope and courage to continue the journey. The LORD is our strength and refuge, and our very present help in such times of need. We will find His help as we continue relentlessly in sharing His word on His altar and pray daily. Our children too, will learn to deal with issues of life from what they learn from us. They shall surely be blessed with the blessings of Abraham, which will continue with the next generation.

CONCLUSION

This book is written for Christian couples. Until one becomes born-again, he cannot live by the standard of the word of God. An unregenerate man cannot understand the things of God, and so cannot build the home I described in this book. I therefore encourage everyone that has read this book, who desires to become a member of the family of God, and enjoy the fullness and resources of salvation and the blessings of God to please pray this prayer:

Dear Heavenly Father, I thank You for giving me the LORD Jesus to be my LORD and my Savior. I confess that I am a sinner, and I cannot save myself from my sins. I believe in my heart that the LORD Jesus died for my sins, and that He was raised from the dead for my justification. Today LORD Jesus, I invite you into my heart to be my LORD and my Savior. Every agreement I have with Satan; I cancel it today in Jesus name.

The word of God says in Romans 10:9 that if you confess with your mouth the LORD Jesus, and believe in your heart that God raised him from the dead, you will be saved. Also, in 2 Corinthians 5: 17, it is written that if anyone is in Christ, he is a new creation; old things are passed away, behold all things have become new. If you meant it when you prayed the above prayers, confessing the LORD Jesus as your LORD and Savior, and believing in your heart that God raised Him from the dead, according to the word of God, you are saved. Congratulations and welcome to the family of God.

Other books by the Author

The Messianic Temple: The LORD is There
(*Ezekiel's Vision of the Third Temple*).

God Hears, God Answers

The Heartbeat Of God: Salvation Of Lost Souls

How Do We Invest In Our Children?

Raising Godly Children: Foundation Laid In Prayers

God Of War, Arise! Battles Belong To The LORD

Elijah: The Prophet Of Fire (Illustrated Youth
Ministry Bible Study Curriculum)

Heroes Of Faith: Lessons And Life
Application/Workbooks
(*For Children and Youth Ministry*).

Lessons And Life Applications Of The Parables Of
Jesus (*Illustrated Sunday School Curriculum For Youth
And Adults*).

Restoration Of Igbo-Jews To Their Prophetic
Destiny: Igbos (Ebo-Hebrews) as the Firstborn

Before You Get Married

www.ingramcontent.com/pod-product-compliance
Lightning Source LLC
Chambersburg PA
CBHW060300050426
42448CB00009B/1705